In Search of
Julian of Norwich

Sheila Upjohn

MOREHOUSE PUBLISHING

An imprint of Church Publishing Incorporated
Harrisburg—New York

Printed in the United States of America

07 08 09 10 11 12 13   10 9 8 7 6 5 4 3 2 1

In Search of
Julian of Norwich

*This book is for my husband Simon
and for The Julian Shrine in Norwich
The Order of Julian of Norwich,
Racine, Wisconsin, USA
The Sisters of the Love of God,
Fairacres, Oxford
whose prayers made it possible*

Contents

Acknowledgements

I am most grateful to Alan Oldfield for permission to use the detail from his painting 'The Ascent of the Servant' for the cover. I am also grateful to SLG Press for permission to quote from *Julian Reconsidered* by Sister Benedicta Ward SLG and to the British Library for permission to reproduce illustrations from the Luttrell Psalter and a MS page from Julian's *Revelations*. The Despencer retable and the boss are reproduced by kind permission of the Dean and Chapter of Norwich Cathedral, and the illustration from the cover of *A Lesson of Love* by Fr John-Julian by permission of Walker and Company.

🌫 1 🌫
The case of the missing manuscripts

In 1973, many people in Norwich found themselves in an embarrassing situation. It was not a discreditable event that caused their discomfiture, quite the reverse. On 8 May 1973 a distinguished company from all over the world gathered in Norwich Cathedral for a celebration.

Back in those days, the people of Norwich were astonished to find that it wasn't purely a Church of England affair. Roman Catholics, many of them priests, monks and nuns, had come from America and France and Italy to pray beside all kinds of churchmen, from all over the world, at a Eucharist celebrated by an Anglican priest. The Chairman of the District Methodist Church of East Anglia was there, and so was the Abbé of Bec. It was the first time, as far as anyone knew, that a Roman Catholic priest had been officially present at a Eucharist in the cathedral since Henry VIII had dissolved the priory in 1538.

The Anglican Bishop of Norwich and the Roman Catholic Bishop of East Anglia sat side by side (though tucked away in a corner, so that, in those adventurous days, they did not have to be seen to give their official blessing to the proceedings).

All this the people of Norwich heard of and approved, but their discomfort grew. The reason was this. The celebration was to honour the 600th anniversary of Julian of

Norwich – and most of them had to admit that they had never even heard the name.

Who was this man? And how had the inhabitants of his native city remained unaware of his existence for 600 years?

Their embarrassment became acute when it was revealed to them that their ignorance was deeper than they had supposed. Julian, it seemed, was not a man after all, but a woman – a woman who had lived in Norwich 600 years before and had written a book.

It became even harder to understand. Norwich is proud of its local heroes. Nelson is honoured every year, and so is Edith Cavell. Amelia Opie and Elizabeth Fry are both remembered. The pictures of Cotman and Crome have pride of place in the city art gallery. George Borrow comes to mind whenever the wind blows on the heath and the statue of Sir Thomas Browne contemplates a broken urn as he sits by the church of St Peter Mancroft in the Haymarket.

Heroes, reformers, painters, writers – all of them local – all are loved and respected. How had Julian been overlooked?

Finding the answer is a detective story where everything is speculation and there are no neat answers in the final chapter. This book, and all the others about Julian, are peppered with the phrases 'it may be', 'it seems probable', 'we can suppose' in every variation that pen can devise.

For almost nothing is known about Julian – not the day she was born, not when she died, not even her real name. But she did write a book and that book remained almost unheard of until centuries after her death. Why?

First we must jump back in time, not quite as far as Norwich in 1373, but to what is, for most of us, an island of fairly firm ground in the morass of English history – back to Henry VIII.

Thanks to Holbein we know what he looked like. Thanks to his womanising we know about his six wives. And thanks to his celebrated divorce from the first of them we know about the break with Rome and the dissolution of the monasteries.

But Julian lived in the 1300s. Why should a king who reigned 200 years later be able to tell us anything at all about her?

When Henry VIII dissolved the monasteries, he swept away a complex system of property, of worship and of learning that had been an almost unchanging part of English life for 500 years. Not since the Norman Conquest had there been an upheaval on this scale. And, like all successful takeovers, it was extremely well documented. Henry's assessors visited all the religious houses in the whole country and noted their value, down to the last farthing. Their bookkeeping is exemplary, and it survives.

The records of the monastic establishments will help us with Julian because one of the few things we are fairly certain of is that, when she wrote her book, she was living at St Julian's church in King Street, and so she was part of an ecclesiastical establishment that had changed very little by the time Henry VIII swept it away some 200 years later.

It is important, too, because the dissolution of the monasteries is the key to why it took several hundred years for Julian's book to become known.

The monasteries were the centres of learning, home to the men and women who could read and write, and they housed the great libraries of England. And at the dissolution of the monasteries those libraries were broken up.

Henry himself got his hands on some of the books. The list of the 600 books in the library at Rochester, drawn up by his men, still survives. Beside the titles of 100 of them are the crosses Henry made with his own hand to indicate those he wanted for his son's library.

Some of the books from the monasteries survive, but an enormous proportion of the harvest of learning that had been gathered in was scattered and destroyed.

Now, one of the things we are certain of is that Julian wrote a book. And we can suppose that her original manuscript (if, indeed, she wrote it down herself and did not dictate it) was itself copied and re-copied by scribes. And we should probably be right in thinking that, 200 years later, copies of her book might have found their way into some of the libraries of some of the religious houses – perhaps only in Norwich, perhaps elsewhere in the country.

What happened to them at the dissolution? The gorgeous missals, gospels and psalters, the gold leaf heavy on their pages, would be targets for looters. But a small plain book, written not in Latin but in common English, would be one of the first to be thrown onto the bonfire. Who would bother to save it?

But somebody did.

In England at the dissolution there were religious orders from all over Europe. When the monasteries were closed they took what possessions they could and fled back to their mother houses in their own countries. Some members of the English communities went with them. And, among all the fugitives, one of them must have taken a copy of Julian's book.

I say 'must have' more than 'might have' because we know for a fact that there was a manuscript copy in the Bibliothèque Nationale in Paris in the 1660s. There is nothing to show how it got there, but it seemed more than likely that it crossed the Channel in the luggage of a monk or a nun. The date of the manuscript, too, looked

We know almost nothing about Julian – not the day she was born,
not when she died, not even her real name. But we do know she
wrote a book. This picture – and most of the others in this book –
are from the Luttrell Psalter, written in East Anglia in Julian's
lifetime. (*Luttrell f.59*)

as though it might even have been brought back by the scribe who copied it.

And then we reach a further mystery. Recently it has been established that this manuscript is 100 years later than was first thought. It was made in the 1600s, copying the style of a manuscript made a century before. We do not know who made it nor where is the original it was copied from.

But at last one solid fact comes into the story in the person of an English Benedictine monk called Serenus de Cressy. In the mid 1600s he was in Paris as chaplain to a newly-founded convent of Benedictine nuns at Cambrai. And while he was there, it seems, he came across the Julian manuscript in the Bibliothèque Nationale.

Certainly in 1670, with the permission of his abbot, he brought out the first-ever printed edition of Julian's book, based on the Paris manuscript.

It would be nice to record that it was an overnight success. But in England in 1670 they were still rejoicing in the Restoration of the monarchy ten years before. The theatres were open once again after 11 years of Puritan repression. Christmas could be celebrated once more, and silks and satins were no longer sinful. It is small wonder that the appearance in print of a small book written by a Norwich woman some 300 years earlier passed almost unnoticed.

But at least, after 300 years, Julian's book had appeared in print. It took nearly 200 years for it to happen again. The man who made it possible, though he did not know it, was Sir Hans Sloane.

If you have ever managed to squeeze your car into a parking space in Hans Place behind Harrods, or strolled down Sloane Street to Sloane Square in what is now Sloane Ranger territory, you will have trodden in the footsteps of Sir Hans Sloane. For it was he, distinguished physician and scientist that he was, who bought the Manor of Chelsea in 1712, not to set up a chain of boutiques, but to establish a botanic garden there – the Chelsea Physic Garden.

He was a renowned collector, and he collected other people's collections, too. He collected drawings and paintings, coins and medals, zoological and geological specimens – and above all he collected books and manuscripts. When he died in 1753, he left his collection to the nation on condition that Parliament should pay his executors £20,000 – a bargain at the price.

It was the start of the British Museum. And there among the manuscripts, though no one knew it at the time, were two copies of Julian's book.

But although the nation bought the Sloane collection in 1753, it took another 100 years before there was a printed edition from the British manuscript. In 1877 the Revd Henry Collins brought out the first-ever edition from one of the Sloane manuscripts. Before then, in 1843, Serenus de Cressy's edition was reprinted.

Neither of them, as far as we can tell, had very many readers.

And yet books are mysterious things. In the days before paperbacks in England (and soon this will be beyond living memory) many of the cheap editions of the classics used in schools were the *King's Treasuries of Literature* series. They are small books, not much bigger than a Beatrix Potter, and on their endpapers are Milton's words from his great speech in defence of freedom of the press: 'A good book is the precious lifeblood of a master spirit.' The whole of that quotation runs: 'A good book is the precious lifeblood of a master spirit, embalmed and treasured up on purpose for a life beyond life.'

Julian's book is surely the precious lifeblood of a master spirit, but it is pulsing with life, not embalmed. And certainly it seems to have been treasured up on purpose for a life centuries beyond her own. Its influence today is incalculable. And who can calculate its influence on those who have read it in the past, no matter how few their numbers may have been?

We know the name of one of them. Florence Nightingale took Julian's book to the Crimea with her and read it amid the blood and suffering of Scutari Hospital.

So the years went by and still, after more than 500 years, Julian's voice had yet to be heard in the twentieth century. The person who made it possible is once more a woman, and once more someone about whom we can discover very little.

In 1901 Methuen brought out an edition of Julian's book from one of the Sloane manuscripts (the second had not yet come to light). It was edited by a 46-year-old woman who had never published a book before. Her name was Grace Warrack.

Methuen could hardly have expected to find themselves with a best-seller on their hands, but the plain fact of the matter is that Grace Warrack's edition was reprinted and reprinted again for the next 70 years. It was never out of print even through two world wars.

Who was the woman who brought Julian's book so triumphantly into the twentieth century?

Like so many of the people in this book, we know almost nothing about her. Her publishers have no information, and all I have been able to find comes from an entry in *Who Was Who* (a sad title if ever there was one).

'Unmarried, third daughter of the late John Warrack, born in Aberdeen in 1855, lived in Edinburgh, died 1932'. It tells us nothing about the kind of person she was nor, even more tantalising, how she acquired the knowledge she needed to edit the text.

Entries for men on the same page have a subhead 'educ'.

[8]

One of them reads 'Eton and RMA Sandhurst', another 'Clifton College and scholar of Balliol'. But there's no 'educ' entry for Grace Warrack, not even 'privately'.

She lived in Edinburgh, so the chances are she got her training there. But women weren't admitted to Edinburgh University until 1892, when she was 37. There is no record of her taking a degree, or even matriculating. It's possible that she attended classes run by the Edinburgh Association for University Education for Women.

So there she is, the third daughter of the late John Warrack, who out of the blue, at the age of 46, produces this amazing book: a solid piece of independent research with excellent footnotes and cross-references and, above all, a wonderful feeling for the strengths and rhythms of Julian's prose.

It is through Grace Warrack that Julian's book first became known in the twentieth century. And so Norwich citizens can be comforted that their ignorance is not as long-standing as they had originally supposed. For it is effectively, not for 600 years, but only since the beginning of this century that it has been possible to lay hands on a copy.

Today it is easy to come by. There is a choice of editions and translations (for her English, the English of Chaucer's time, needs updating to be understood) and nearly every library and religious bookshop has a copy on its shelves.

But before we take it down and open it, let us try to piece together a picture of the kind of life Julian led, and the conditions under which she wrote.

2

The scene of the crime

England in the fourteenth century seems, at least from our viewpoint in the twentieth century, to be a picturesque and untroubled place.

It was the age of chivalry, of Chaucer; the age of pilgrimage and of pageantry; the age where formal daisies bejewelled the grass at the feet of unicorns; the age that was to inspire the Pre-Raphaelites and bring romance to temper the hustling efficiency of the Victorian iron age.

Norwich in the fourteenth century was a city of consequence – no provincial backwater but the second city in England. It was the centre of a rich agricultural district; a producer, a manufacturer and an exporter. Norfolk wool was famous, and so was Norfolk weaving. Its fine worsted cloth was to become the envy of Europe.

Early in the century, England blundered into war with France – a plan by the Pope to unite the rivals in a joint Crusade having come to grief. The war was to drain the country's resources, but in the early stages there were gains, particularly for Norwich.

The English longbowmen won the battle of Crécy in 1346 and the following year took Calais – which was to remain an English possession for nearly 200 years, until its loss by Mary Tudor engraved its name on her heart.

But, Calais apart, the coast of France was hostile and the southern ports of England, opposite the enemy shore, were open to attack. Not so Norwich.

Norfolk lies across the Channel from the Low Countries and, as the ports in the south became more dangerous, trade flooded into Norwich. The city lies, not exposed on the coast, but 30 miles of navigable river upstream from Yarmouth. Not since the days of the Viking longships had it been vulnerable to attack.

Masons were at work building Norwich cathedral cloisters when Julian was writing her book. One of them left a self-portrait on a roof boss.
(*Norwich Cathedral*)

Trade was booming. Bales of goods, the local wool and cloth among them, were shipped out of Norwich to friendly Flanders and the Rhineland. Back came Rhenish wine and Flemish lace. The network of roads and waterways led inland from Norwich to London, Lincoln and York.

Craftsmen came, too. Skilled weavers came from Flanders to help weave the local wool. Master masons and glaziers came to help build the churches that were springing up thick and fast as local merchants sought to put at least part of their profits into an investment that could be to their long-term – preferably their eternal – advantage.

Norwich in those days was a walled city, a packed square mile with some 6,000 citizens secure within the protection of its barred gates and fortified flint walls.

It was a crowded square mile. Medieval cities were neither segregated nor sanitary. Cheek by jowl the people lived with their hens and goats, their pigs and dogs. Open drains ran through the streets. The blood from the slaughterhouses stank in the streets beside the stench of the tanneries and tallowmakers. The breweries and dyehouses took water from the river alongside the fish wharves and the shipyards. The dung heaps were beside the parish pump, and the parish pump took water from the well sunk beside the graveyard.

In this square mile there were hovels and palaces, mansions and market booths. And, above all, there were churches.

Norwich today has 32 surviving medieval churches within its city walls, a number which its twentieth-century citizens regard as an embarrassment of riches, and for which, worship being out of fashion, they strive to find 'suitable secular uses'.

But in Julian's day there were many more churches in the square mile of Norwich, most of them brand, spanking new – and more being built on all sides. And, as if this were not enough, there were the monasteries and convents – 22 of them inside the city walls and another eight in the fields beyond.

Down on the river meadows lay the biggest of them all, the Benedictine priory with the old Norman cathedral

When the artist of the Luttrell Psalter (made in East Anglia while
Julian was alive) wanted to draw a picture of Constantinople, he
took an example from near at home. Although it is captioned as
Constantinople the city is clearly the walled city of Norwich,
complete with cathedral spire – topped by the weathercock – and
hospitable inn signs. (*Luttrell f.164b*)

at its heart, founded by the Norman bishop de Losinga
some three centuries before. Here, too, the builders were
at work, rebuilding the spire, blown down in the tremen-
dous gales of 1362, and taking advantage of the oppor-
tunity to rebuild the damaged east end in the new style.

The cloisters, begun at the beginning of the century,
were growing under the masons' hammers, and big
square-headed windows were being opened up in the
triforium to let in more light.

There were 60 monks at the cathedral priory at the
dissolution, but the number of people employed must
have run into hundreds. The list on page 14 (from Henry
VIII's *Valor Ecclesiasticus*) shows the scope of the operation,
from the keeper of the shrines and the infirmarian, down
to the swanherd and the porter of the fishhouse.

Being a part of the religious establishment in Norwich
in the fourteenth century must have been even less
remarkable than working for the Norwich Union is in the
city today.

[13]

The establishment of the convent, before the Dissolution, consisted of the following persons, officers, &c.

The lord prior.	Carpenter.
The sub-prior.	Porter of the cellar.
Sixty monks.	Porter of the fish-house.
Sacrist.	Caterer.
Sub-sacrist.	Woodherds.
Cellarer or bursar.	Gardener's men.
Sub-cellarer or butler.	The monks' servants (more than
Camerarius or Chamberlain.	60).
Almoner.	Janitor or porter.
Refectorer.	Keeper of the sanctuarium.
Pittancier.	Granarii, keepers of the garners.
Chaplains.	Gardeners.
Precentor or chantor.	Tokener.
Sub-chantor.	Hostilarii or grooms.
Infirmarer.	Stallarius.
Choristers.	Provendarius.
Keeper of the shrines.	The swanherd.
Lay Officers.	Carcerarius or gaoler.
Prior's butler.	Grangearii or grangers.
Cellarer's butler.	Servants of the larder.
Clerk of the infirmary.	Servants of the kitchen.
Miller.	Carters.
Cooper.	Scullions.
Maltster.	&c. &c.

As well as the churches and the religious houses there were 37 guild chapels, a cell for a hermit in each of the ten city gates, and 36 anchorages.

An anchorage might perhaps sound the sort of thing you would expect to find in the flourishing port of Norwich, but these anchorages had nothing to do with boats. They were small houses, usually built against the wall of a church, which housed an anchorite or an anchoress.

Some of these men and women would be monks and nuns, but many were just ordinary men and women who took vows to live a solitary life of prayer and meditation.

It was not a life that everyone was suited to. It would have a dangerous attraction for inadequates who wanted to be shut away from a world they could not cope with – and it could also be seen as a soft option by those who thought the haven of a cell would provide a refuge from the rigours and discipline of the monastic life or the cares of the world.

Then, as now, no one could become a solitary on their own say-so. Would-be anchoresses were rigorously examined by their own superiors, if they were monks and nuns, and by their bishop to see whether they had a vocation to the solitary life.

Now, one of the few facts we know about Julian is that she was one of the anchoresses of Norwich and, though we do not know for certain whether or not she was a professed nun, we do know that for a large part of her life she lived in an anchorage at St Julian's church in King Street. It was there she wrote her book.

How did an anchoress live and how did she pass her time?

We can make some assumptions with the help of a book written some hundred years before Julian's time – the *Ancrene Riwle*, or Anchoresses' Rule Book.

It was written for the guidance of three enclosed Sisters near Salisbury, possibly by their bishop and, unlike most religious books of the period it was, like Julian's book, written in English. It shows that an anchoress, enclosed though she might be, did not live in some kind of ethereal limbo. Take, for example, this advice about clothes:

'Be content with your clothes, whether they are white or black – only see they are plain, and warm, and well made – skins well tanned; and have as many as you need – for bed and also for back. . . Let your shoes be thick and warm.'

Many households in the city would have a house cow,

but an anchoress is warned against it: 'My dear sisters, you should keep no beast except a cat. An anchoress that has cattle seems more like a housewife, as Martha was, than an anchoress. . . For then you must think about cow's fodder, of the herdsman's wages, must keep in with the town herdsman, go to law when the cow is impounded and, perhaps, pay damages. . . An anchoress should have nothing that draws her heart outwards.'

If Julian lived according to the *Ancrene Riwle*, her cell would have had three windows. One would open into the church so she could hear the Mass and receive the sacrament. A second window opened onto an inner room, so that a servant could bring food and clean clothes, and take out the slops. The third window, which was curtained by a black cloth with a white cross at the centre, opened onto the roadway, so the anchoress could look out into the world and speak with people who came in need of her counsel and help.

Another writer of a book of rules for recluses, Aelred of Rievaulx, writing some 200 years before Julian, gives a vivid picture of how an anchoress should not behave when she speaks through her window on the world:

> At her window will be seated some garrulous old gossip pouring idle tales into her ears, feeding her with scandal and gossip; describing in detail the face, appearance and mannerisms of now this priest, now that monk or clerk; describing too the frivolous behaviour of a young girl; the free and easy ways of a widow who thinks what she likes is right; the cunning ways of a wife who cuckolds her husband while she gratifies her passions. The recluse all the while is dissolved in laughter, loud peals of laughter.

But the window on the world and counselling those who came was an important part of a solitary's function.

When St Cuthbert was living as a hermit on the remote island of Farne, people came on pilgrimage to see him from all over the country. 'They told him the sins they had committed, or the temptations of devils that had beset them, or else told of the common troubles of mankind that burdened them, hoping they would get consolation from a man of such holiness. Nor were their hopes in vain. For nobody went away from him without consolation, and no one took away with him the sorrow he had brought there,' Bede tells us.

Yet sometimes for a solitary the demands of people at the window must have been as irksome as the telephone is today. There must have often been a temptation to feel that the troubles clamouring outside should take second place to the work of prayer to which they had vowed their life. Walter Hilton, who lived at the same time as Julian, had some advice on the subject:

Since you ought not to go out of your house to seek occasion how you may profit your neighbours by deeds of charity, because you are enclosed. . . Therefore, who so will speak to you. . . be you soon ready with a good will to ask what his will is. . . for you know not what he is, nor why he comes, nor what need he has of you, or you of him, till you have tried. And though you be at prayer, or at your devotions, that you think loth to break off, for that you think that you ought not to leave God to speak with anyone, I think not so in this case, for if you be wise, you shall not leave God, but you shall find Him, and have Him, and see Him in your neighbour. . .

If he come to tell you his distress or trouble, and to be comforted by your speech, hear him gladly, and suffer him to say what he will for ease of his own heart. And when he has done, comfort him if

[17]

you can, gladly, gently and charitably, and soon break off. And then, after that, if he will fall into idle tales, or vanities of the World, or of other men's actions, answer him but little, and feed not his speech, and he will soon be weary and quickly take his leave.

Anchoresses would say the Offices, the official prayers of the church, at their proper times, starting with Lauds at daybreak. They would read and write, if they were literate, and might also mend church linen. But most of their time would be spent in meditation and prayer.

Most of them, even some members of religious orders, would have to have money of their own to buy food and clothes for themselves and for their servant. The money often came from bequests.

We know that Julian was left money by Roger Reed, the rector of St Michael's church at Coslany in 1393. Twenty-two years later John Plumpton left 40 pence to Julian and 12 pence each to Alice, her former serving maid, and to her present servant. There was another bequest a year later in 1416.

At that date, Julian would have been 74 or 75 – a ripe old age in the fourteenth century – but a mention in Blomefield's *History of Norwich* of 'Julian the ankress' in 1443 is unlikely to be our Julian, still alive at over 100 years old. It is more likely to be the anchoress who took over the cell after Julian's death.

It was no coincidence that she, too, was called Julian. Once an anchoress entered her cell, it was usual for her to give up her own name and simply be known by the name of the church she lived by. What Julian's real name was, we shall never know.

Many people must have brought their joys and troubles to Julian's window on the world in the 40 or so years she lived in King Street. And, by great good fortune, one of them also wrote a book, and has left us a firsthand account of their meeting. Her name was Margery Kempe.

৩ 3 ৩

The evidence of an eyewitness

Margery Kempe, like Julian, was a Norfolk woman and was born in 1373 in the prosperous seaport of King's Lynn (then Bishop's Lynn) on the north Norfolk coast.

Her book, discovered only in 1934 and called simply *The Book of Margery Kempe*, is the earliest surviving autobiography in English. Margery had to dictate her book to a scribe because, like most laymen and women in the fourteenth century, she could not read or write.

Margery was a very devout woman, and one result of this was that she was visited by the 'gift of tears', a gift which she shared with several other medieval holy women. It was a gift that was not without its drawbacks.

When she thought of Christ's Passion, whether she was in church or in the street, she would burst into loud sobbing and wailing which she was quite unable to contain or control. It did not endear her to her companions.

She went on pilgrimages and travelled to the Holy Land, and to Assisi, Rome, Danzig, Norway and Santiago de Compostela. On these pilgrimages her long-suffering fellow-travellers, appalled by the noise she made, avoided her whenever they could, crept off and left her to find her own way home from foreign cities, and even changed ships when they saw her coming.

But priests who took the trouble to spend time with her became convinced that her weeping was something outside her control, and that the gift of tears was genuine.

One priest, the man who was later to write down the book at Margery's dictation, had a disconcerting demonstration of the gift:

> And our Lord also visited the priest when at mass with such grace and devotion when he should read the Holy Gospel that he wept amazingly, so that he wetted his vestments and the ornaments of the altar, and could not control his weeping or his sobbing, it was so abundant; nor could he restrain it, or very well stand at the altar because of it.
>
> Then he well believed that the good woman, for whom he had previously had little affection, could not restrain her weeping, her sobbing, nor her crying, and that she felt much more abundance of grace than ever he did, beyond comparison.

But many people remained unconvinced, including a

Margery Kempe, a Norfolk woman from King's Lynn, came to Norwich to ask Julian's advice. Margery also wrote a book, but had to dictate it to a scribe because she could not read and write. The manuscript of her book, with its account of her meeting with Julian, disappeared – as did Julian's – and was rediscovered only in 1934. (*Luttrell (B) f.74*)

[21]

well-known preacher in her home town of Lynn. He turned her out of the church, preached against her, and turned a great many people against her.

Margery herself bore all this as well as she could, but needed to ask someone for advice. She went to Norwich to consult Julian about her experiences: 'which she described to the anchoress to find out if there were any deception in them, for the anchoress was expert in such things and could give good advice.'

Julian advised her 'to be obedient to the will of our Lord and fulfil with all her might whatever he put in her soul, if it were not against the worship of God and the profit of her fellow-Christians. For if it were, then it were not the influence of a good spirit, but rather of an evil spirit. . . '

> Set all your trust in God and do not fear the talk of the world, for the more contempt, shame and reproof that you have in this world, the more is your merit in the sight of God. Patience is necessary for you, for in that you shall keep your soul.

Margery apparently stayed in Norwich for some days, for she reports:

'Great was the holy conversation that the anchoress and this creature [as Margery always refers to herself] had through talking of the love of our Lord Jesus Christ for the many days they were together.'

It says a great deal for Margery Kempe and the integrity of her gift that Julian was prepared to spend so much time at the outer window speaking with her.

ꙮ 4 ꙮ

Death and destruction

Most of the people who brought their troubles to Julian
would be burdened more by 'the common troubles of
mankind' than by the spiritual dilemmas that beset Margery Kempe. And in fourteenth-century Norwich there
were troubles in plenty. The first was the long-drawn-out
war with France.

Behind it lay the fact that the English Plantagenet kings
had huge possessions in France. It had all begun when
Eleanor of Aquitaine married Henry II, after her marriage
to the Dauphin, which had produced two daughters, was
annulled.

By Julian's day the kings of England had also been
dukes of Aquitaine for nearly 200 years – an arrangement
not unpopular with the people of Aquitaine, who pre-
ferred an absentee duke in England to an ever-present king
in Paris with his tax-collectors. But clearly it did not suit
the king of France.

The war that began in 1338 was to drag on inconclus-
ively for more than 100 years. (Henry V almost brought
it to a successful conclusion when, after Agincourt, he
married Katherine of France and they jointly produced an
heir to both kingdoms. But Henry's death from trench
fever two years later threw the whole thing back in the
melting-pot.)

When the war began, Edward III's aim was simply to
hold on to the territory he owned in France, but soon,

for political reasons, he was laying claim to the throne of France itself, to which he was manifestly not entitled. The demands of the war, in taxes and men, grew throughout the century. Few Englishmen could see the purpose of it.

The results were plain to see. The country grew poorer, shipping was attacked, and England's old enemy Scotland, which had signed an alliance with France, invaded from the north and reached Durham before their army was defeated.

All this was far away from Norwich, but in 1348, when Julian must have been about five years old, events turned nearer home. There was a disastrous outbreak of a highly-infectious cattle disease in Norfolk. And much worse was to come the following year.

The Black Death, which had begun in Dorset, reached Norwich in January 1349. It was a disease that struck without warning. There were no early symptoms, no lengthy illness – and, above all, no treatment. People who rose hale and hearty in the morning could be dead by nightfall. Estimates put the number of dead in this epidemic and the two that followed it at about 2,400 out of a population of 6,000.

There is no precise record of how many people died in Norfolk and Norwich during the Black Death, partly because soon there was no one left to keep up the parish registers. The priests, called day and night from one death-bed to another, were among the chief casualties. In one parish three new vicars were installed in two months, and a hard-pressed Bishop Despencer wrote to the Pope asking for permission to ordain men aged 21 instead of 24.

Soon there were not enough priests to administer the last rites and, in the anguish of bereavement, the survivors were tortured by the added fear that those they loved, having died unshriven – without confessing their sins and receiving absolution – would burn forever in eternal torment.

The passing bell rang throughout the day and at night-fall the death carts were pushed through the streets with the cry of 'Bring out your dead'.

The bodies of husbands, wives and children would be dragged out and heaved unceremoniously onto the cart to be taken away and tipped into mass graves. The swollen churchyards mounted higher and higher above the level of the streets until there was scarcely a street in the city without the plague cross daubed on its doors.

Thirteen years later, in 1362, when Julian would have been 19, the plague came back. This time it seemed like a massacre of the innocents. The plague claimed most of its victims among young children. That year, too, there was a great gale that blew down the cathedral spire, tore up trees and damaged houses. The following year, cattle disease broke out once more.

When Julian was 26, there was a threefold disaster. The Black Death raged again in the city and county, cattle disease was rampant, and, to cap it all, after years of bad harvests, the harvest of 1369 was the worst for 50 years.

Where once there was simply hunger, starvation now stalked the streets of the city and the Norfolk countryside. Landowners, faced with poverty themselves, struggled to keep serfs tied to the land and wages down. The long-drawn-out war still needed ever more money and men.

The result, born of hunger and desperation, was the Peasants' Revolt.

The rebels stormed Norwich and the gates were opened for them. They took over the castle and staged mock trials – followed by genuine executions. They looted the churches and despoiled the monasteries.

In the county, the rebels were savagely and effectively put down by Henry Despencer, the battling bishop of

Norwich. He intercepted and killed the messenger the Norwich rebels had sent to London to ask pardon from the king, and rode back into the city to take control. (The glorious painting he gave to celebrate his victory is still in Norwich Cathedral.)

Litster, the leader of the rebels, was caught as he tried to escape, tied by his heels behind a horse, and dragged through the cobbled streets of the city. He was tried before the Bishop and sentenced to death. Then he was publicly hanged and, equally publicly, drawn and quartered.

How could the misery, dirt and violence of fourteenth-century Norwich have produced a woman whose most famous words are 'All shall be well'?

Perhaps, we may suppose, it was because she was a woman of great faith, and so she was able to draw strength and comfort from the bedrock of the universal Church, as yet a couple of centuries away from the upheavals and doubts of the Reformation.

But Julian's lifetime also saw the start of what is now called the Great Schism, the great rift in the Roman Catholic Church which led to the scandalous spectacle of two rival popes, one in Avignon and one in Rome.

The scandal was compounded by the fact that the Rome contender, Urban VI, anxious to defeat his rival at all

---

Julian could have known this altarpiece of the crucifixion, given to the cathedral by her bishop, Henry Despencer. It is still there today because of the ingenuity of someone whose name we shall never know. When the image-breakers (Henry VIII's looters or Cromwell's Roundheads) approached the cathedral, he turned the picture face downwards, put legs on it, and made it into a table. So it remained until one day in 1847 a member of the Archaeological Institute, meeting in the cathedral, dropped his pencil. As he crawled under the table to retrieve it, he looked up – and found himself gazing at a masterpiece. The illustration shows the centre panel.
(*Norwich Cathedral*)

costs, raised money for a military campaign by selling indulgences. This was common practice, until Martin Luther took his stand on it some century and a half later, and the notion that money given to the Church could buy remission of time in purgatory was well established.

But Urban VI went one better. He promised remission of time in purgatory for the relatives of those who contributed, even if they had been dead for years. Perhaps he had his eye on the market of those whose loved ones had died unshriven during the plague years.

One of the first to answer the call to arms was Bishop Despencer of Norwich. He set off to lead a Crusade against the Avignon Pope. His army was defeated and the survivors struggled home, looting as they went.

The scandals in the Church were enough to shake the faith of its most loyal supporters. John Wycliff, the scholar and theologian, attacked the papacy, calling it Antichrist itself. Despencer led the campaign against him and pressed for (and got) the threat of the death penalty.

In the event, Wycliff escaped being burnt at the stake. He died peacefully at his country rectory. The worst his enemies could do was to dig up his body and fling it in the river. But hundreds of his followers were not so fortunate.

In the years that followed, men, women and children were tried in Norwich Cathedral, week by week, and then led in procession down Bishopgate and over Bishop's Bridge. On the waste ground beyond the city boundary they were tied to stakes and brushwood was piled round them in the Lollards Pit. The crime of some of them was to own a Bible translated into English.

The smoke from their burning would have drifted into Julian's cell on the north-east wind.

It is against this background that we must examine Julian's book and her assurance that all shall be well.

❧ 5 ☙
The events of eighth May

So far we have made a voyage round Julian's book. It is high time to take it off the shelf and find out what it is about and why she wrote it.

Julian wrote her book because, on 8 May 1373, she had a vision.

It's at this point that one senses a distinct slackening of interest. For while it is all very well to paint a picture of a time and place one has never visited, it is far less acceptable to describe a state of mind one has never entered.

But Julian's book will take us beyond the usual range of our thinking. It will take us as far as reason and logic can carry us, and will lead us on to explore territory beyond.

One of the drawbacks of the twentieth century is that we have become unused to handling anything except scientific evidence. We seem almost to have forgotten that something can be true even though it cannot be scientifically proved.

We have become unfamiliar with the pursuit of truth as opposed to the checking of facts. It is a pursuit in which the quarry is stationary and it is only we who move, changing our route, our speed and our angle of approach.

The pursuit of truth must consider love. There is no way to prove, or test, or measure love. Yet the working of love is far more important than, say, the scientifically-proven first law of thermodynamics. Pain and grief with their destructive (and, surprisingly, their healing) powers resist being analysed and quantified, yet their effect on our lives is more significant than, say, the measurable effect of our intake of cholesterol.

Our perception of God – or our failure to perceive God at all – and our consequent assumptions about the nature of each other and of the world we live in, governs everything we think and do.

Our efforts to perceive God must take us beyond what can be physically observed and what can be checked by logic and reason. This does not mean we are free simply to abandon their rules and believe whatever we care to imagine. We must apply the rules as far as they take us, and acknowledge when they reach their limits.

Julian is aware of this when she describes what she calls her 'showings'. They reached her in three ways – by physical sight, by words that came into her mind, and by spiritual insight. She describes the sights and records the words with meticulous accuracy. But she knows that spiritual insight must reach people individually and cannot be passed on in its entirety from one person to another:

'The spiritual sight I do not know how, nor am I able, to show it as openly or as fully as I wish,' she reports. But what she can describe in full, she sets down with great accuracy:

When I was thirty-and-a-half years old, God sent me an illness which held me three days and three nights. On the fourth night I received all the rites of Holy Church and did not think to live until day. And after this I lingered on two days and two nights. And on the third night I often thought I was dying, and so did those who were with me.

And, young as I was, I thought it was sad to die: not because of anything on earth I wanted to live

iarum fuarum: 1 preualurqin ua

'When I was thirty and a half years old, God sent me an illness which held me three days and three nights. . . and on the third night I often thought I was dying, and so did those who were with me,' Julian wrote. (*Luttrell (C) f.98*)

for, and not because of any pain I was afraid of – for I trusted God's mercy – but because if I had lived I should have been able to love God better and for longer, so that I should know God better and love him more in the joy of heaven.

For I thought that the time I had lived here on earth was too small and too short to deserve that endless joy – it seemed like nothing.

And so I thought: 'Good Lord, if I live no longer, may it be to your glory!'

And I understood in my mind and my body that I should die. And I assented to it with my heart and will, that God's will should be my will.

And so I lasted until day, and by then my body was dead from the waist down, as I felt. Then I asked to be propped upright, leaning on others, so I should have more freedom in my heart to be at God's command and to think on God for as long as my life should last.

My priest was sent for to be at my end, and by the time he came, my eyes were set and I could not speak. He held the cross before me and said: 'I have brought you the likeness of your Maker and Saviour. Look upon it, and draw comfort from it.'

I thought I was doing right, for my eyes were turned upwards to heaven, where I trusted to go by the mercy of God. Nevertheless, I told myself to turn my eyes to the cross if I could, and I did so, even though I had thought that I could look nowhere except upwards.

After this, my sight began to fail and it was all dark around me in the room as if it were night – except for the cross. I saw it glow with light and I did not know how. Everything except the cross was hideous to me, as if it were possessed by devils.

After this, the upper part of my body began to die, so completely that I had hardly any feeling and could scarcely breathe. And then I truly thought I was dying.

At this moment, suddenly all my pain was taken from me and I was as well, particularly in the upper part of my body, as ever I was before. I marvelled at this sudden change, for I thought it was a special work of God and not of nature.

When the pain suddenly left her, Julian remembered something. Years before, she had wanted to experience Christ's crucifixion as if she had actually been at the foot of the cross with his mother and his friends, as Christ hung dying.

We might question, at this point, whether Julian's wish to experience this degree of grief was perverse, perhaps unbalanced. But all Christians have the crucifixion as the central point of their faith. And anyone who has ever been in church on Good Friday has tried to spend at least some time at the foot of the cross.

What we have to discover is whether Julian had an experience that is deeper than anything we have encountered and whether, as a result, she gained an insight that is more profound than anything we have known.

Until the moment when her pain disappeared, Julian had no indication that anything out of the ordinary was happening. But as she looked steadily at the crucifix, as the priest had told her to, the laws of nature were suspended:

> Suddenly I saw the red blood trickle down from under the crown of thorns, hot and fresh and flooding out as it did at the time of his Passion when the crown of thorns was pressed into his blessed head – he who was both God and man and suffered for me.

Julian's experience was more complex than a simple vision of the crucifixion. It was overlaid by other images. She goes on:

> At the same time as I saw this sight of the head bleeding, our Lord showed me an inward sight of his homely loving. I saw that he is everything that is good and comforting to us. He is our clothing, who for love enwraps and holds us. He enfolds us in love and he will never let us go. I saw that he is everything that is good.
>
> And then he showed me a little thing, the size of a hazelnut, in the palm of my hand; and it was as round as a ball. I looked at in my mind's eye and I thought: 'What can this be?' And answer came: 'It is all that is made.' I marvelled that it could last, for I thought it might have crumbled to nothing, it was

[33]

so small. And the answer came into my mind: 'It lasts, and ever shall, because God loves it.' And so all things have being through the love of God.

In this little thing I saw three truths. The first is that God made it; the second is that God loves it; and the third is that God looks after it.

We need to know how small creation is, and to count created things as nothing, if we are to love and have God who is not created. For this is the reason we are not at rest in heart and soul – that here we seek rest in things that are so little there is no rest in them, and we do not know our God who is all mighty, all wise and all good. For he is true rest.

Anyone who sees the restlessness and lack of inner peace that seems to grow daily in the world will have no difficulty in accepting Julian's diagnosis that 'here we seek rest in things that are so little there is no rest in them'.

We seek rest in holidays, in houses, in jobs, in cars, in drugs, in money, and we seek it, above all, in relationships – relationships in which we are neither able to give nor to be given to in full. For it should be blindingly obvious that we cannot give ourselves fully to anyone or anything unless we first discover who we are. You cannot give what you do not possess.

The couches and consulting rooms of psychiatrists are full of people trying to find themselves, seeking an answer to the question 'Who am I?' It is perfectly obvious that we are becoming frighteningly alienated from each other. What is less obvious is that the reason is that we have become alienated from ourselves.

Julian's insight is that our soul is so intricately knitted to God that we cannot know one without knowing the other:

And so I saw full surely that it is easier for us to

come to know God than to know our own soul. For our soul is so deep-rooted in God, and so endlessly treasured, that we cannot come to know it until we first know God, its maker, to whom it is joined. But, in spite of this, I saw that we must, to be complete, wisely and truly desire to know our own soul. And by doing this, we are taught to seek it where it is. And that is, in God.

The idea that man is incomplete without God is hardly a new one. But Julian reaches out to grasp that, if man is incomplete without God, God is incomplete without man.

I would hazard a guess, and in this spiritual detective story we are guessing all the time, that inside the minds of most of us who have been brought up as Christians there is the following scenario:

God the Father created the world and mankind. Because man sinned through his own fault, the Father sent his Son into the world. For this purpose, the Son temporarily took man's nature so that he was able to suffer and to die. He conquered death by rising to life and then, after the ascension, assumed his own Godlike nature once again.

Julian's insight is that Christ did not take our nature temporarily, but permanently. Because of the way God originally made us, and because of the fact that God, in Jesus, entered humanity, our nature, Christ's nature and God's nature are the same:

And I saw no difference between God's substance and our substance, but, as it were, all God. And yet my understanding took it that our substance is contained within God – that is to say, that God is God, and our substance is created by God.

But how can God lack anything? How can he need us? If there is an unquenchable holiness within us, what has

[35]

been able to go so demonstrably and disastrously wrong? How can God not blame us for our failure?

At this point it seems a good idea to stand aside and let Julian speak for herself. What follows is a shortened version of Julian's chapter 51, the longest chapter of her book, which was written after 20 years meditation.

It is the answer she was given to her urgent, anguished entreaty:

> I wondered and was amazed with all the strength of my soul and thought this: 'Good Lord, I see you are truth itself, and I know truly that we sin grievously all the day long and are much to blame. And I can neither forsake knowing this truth, nor do I see you put any blame on us. How can this be?'
>
> For I knew by the daily teaching of Holy Church, and by my own feelings, that the blame for our sins hangs heavy upon us, from the first man until the time we come up to heaven. This, then, was my wonder – that I saw our Lord putting no more blame upon us than if we were as clean and holy as the angels in heaven.
>
> And my mind was greatly troubled, in its blindness, by these two contradictions, and I knew no rest, for fear that his blessed presence should pass from my sight and I should be left not knowing how he looks on us in our sin.
>
> I cried out inwardly with all my strength, reaching into God for help, meaning this: 'Ah, Lord Jesus, king of bliss, how shall I have peace? Who shall teach me and tell me what I need to know, if I cannot see it in you now?'

The answer came in a parable.

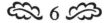

6

The servant's story

Then our courteous Lord answered by showing, very mistily, a wonderful parable of a lord who has a servant.*

The lord sits with dignity, at rest, and in peace. The servant stands reverently before his lord, ready to do his will. The lord looks upon his servant lovingly and tenderly and gently sends him to a certain place to do his bidding. The servant does not simply go, but leaps up and runs off at great speed to do his bidding, because he loves his lord. And then he falls into a gully and is very badly hurt.

And the worst thing I saw befall him was that he had no comfort. For he could not turn his head to look upon his loving lord, from whom all comfort flows.

And I looked carefully to see any blame or fault in him, or if his lord should lay any blame on him, and truly there was none to be seen. For the only reason he fell was because of his good will and his great desire – and he was still as eager and good at heart after he fell as he was when he stood before his lord ready to do his bidding.

And twenty years after the time of the showing, all but three months I was taught inwardly – as I shall set down: 'You must pay close heed to all the circumstances and details that were shown in the parable, even though it seems to you they were obscure and unimportant.'

* This chapter is a shortened version of Julian's chapter 51.

I began by looking at the Lord and the servant, and the way the lord sat, and the place where he sat, the colour of his clothes and their shape; and his outward appearance, and at his nobleness and greatness within. I looked at the way the servant stood, and where and how he stood, at the way he was dressed, the colour and shape of his clothes, at his outward appearance and at his inward goodness and eagerness.

The lord who sat in solemn state, at rest and in peace, I understood is God. The servant who stood before the lord I understand was meant as Adam – that is to say, one man was shown then, and his fall, to make it plain from this how God regards a man and his fall. For in the sight of God all men are one man, and one man is all men.

This man was hurt in his body and made weak, and he was stunned in his mind, because he turned away from looking towards God. But his will was kept whole in God's sight.

And this was the beginning of the teaching I had at that time through which I was able to come to know how he looks upon us in our sin.

And then I saw that it is only pain itself that hurts and grieves us, and that our courteous Lord comforts us and grieves over us. He always looks upon the soul with gladness, loving us, and longing to bring us back into his bliss.

And still I wondered, seeing the lord and servant, as I said before. I saw the lord sit in state, and the servant standing reverently before his lord. There is a twofold meaning in the servant – one outward, the other inward.

Outwardly, he was clad simply as a labourer in his working clothes. And he stood very close to the lord – not directly in front of him but partly to the side, the left side. He was dressed in a white shirt, just one garment, old and shabby, stained with the sweat of his body,

'He was clad simply as a labourer in his working
clothes. . . just one garment, old and shabby,
stained with the sweat of his body, narrow-fitting
and short – about a hand's breadth below the
knee.' This is how Julian describes the servant in
the parable. (*Luttrell f.173*)

narrow-fitting and short (about a hand's breadth below the
knee), threadbare and looking as if it was nearly worn
out, just about to fall into rags and tatters.

The servant stands for the Son, the second person of
the Trinity. And the servant also stands for Adam, that is
to say, all men.

When Adam fell, God's Son fell. For the holy joining
which was made in heaven means that God's Son could

not be separated from Adam, and by Adam I mean all men. Adam fell from life to death in the pit of this miserable world, and after that he fell into hell.

God's Son fell, with Adam, into the depths of the Virgin's womb – who was Adam's fairest daughter. And he did it to take away Adam's blame, both in heaven and on earth – and with great power he fetched him back from hell.

And so Christ was the servant before he came into the world, standing waiting before the Father, at his command, until the time God willed to send him out to do that glorious Deed by which mankind was brought back again to heaven. (That is to say, notwithstanding he is God, equal with the Father as regards his godhead.)

But he stood before the Father as a servant, willing to take all our care upon him, in his foreseen purpose that he would be made man, so as to save man, and fulfil his Father's will.

And then he set off eagerly at his Father's command, taking no thought for himself and his great pain, and at once he fell low into the Virgin's womb.

The white shirt is the flesh; that he had just one garment shows there is nothing between godhead and manhood; the narrowness is poverty; the age comes from Adam's wearing it; the sweat stains are from Adam's labour; the shortness shows the servant's hard work.

And so I saw the Son stand there, saying in his heart: 'Lo, my dear Father. I stand before you in Adam's shirt, all ready to set off and run. I will gladly be on earth to work to your glory when it is your will to send me. How long shall I wait in longing?'

And the way of all those under heaven who shall come there, is the way of longing and desire. And this desire and this longing was shown in the servant standing before

[40]

the lord, and also in this way – by the Son standing before the Father in Adam's old shirt.

Also in this wonderful example I have a key of learning – as it were the beginning of an ABC – by which I can have some understanding of our Lord's meaning. For the secrets of the whole Revelation are hid in it, notwithstanding that all the showings are full of secrets.

Now the lord no longer sits on bare earth in the wilderness, but he sits in the noblest throne that he has made in heaven for his pleasure. Now the Son no longer stands before the Father in awe as a servant, poorly clad and half naked. But he stands directly in front of the Father, richly dressed in flowing glory with a crown of precious richness on his head.

For it was shown that we are his crown – and that crown is the Father's joy, the Son's glory, the Holy Spirit's delight and the endless wondering joy of all who are in heaven.

Now the Son no longer stands before the Father on the lefthand side like a labourer, but he sits at his Father's right hand in everlasting rest and peace. (But it is not meant that the Son sits at the right hand, side by side, like one man sits beside another in this life, for there is no such way of sitting, as I see it, in the Trinity.) But he sits on his Father's right hand, that is to say, in the highest glory of his Father's joy.

Now is the bridegroom, God's son, at peace with his beloved wife, who is the fair maid of endless joy. Now the Son, very God and true man, sits in his city of rest and peace, which his Father has prepared for him by his will, which has no end and no beginning. And the Father is in the Son, and the Holy Ghost in the Father and in the Son.

❧ 7 ❧

The wrath of God

The parable of the lord and the servant came to Julian because she could not understand how we can escape being blamed for our sins. But today sin is an unfashionable concept. For many people it does not exist, since they believe that every kind of 'badness' has been built into us by the bad things that have happened to us in the past.

In order to sin, we have to be able to choose not to sin. If we are programmed from birth by our heredity, our upbringing and our environment, we have no choice about the way we behave. So sin can be dismissed as something thought up by the Church to make us feel guilty.

This means that, for some, the concept of sin has been replaced by the concept of anti-social behaviour – such as being cruel to animals and infringing other people's 'rights'.

But Julian sees sin as something that damages us more than other people. The only sins she mentions by name are impatience and despair – neither of which does much to impinge on other people's pursuit of happiness.

Sin damages us because it comes between us and God, it alienates us from ourselves, it separates us from our true nature and the joy that is our inheritance.

Julian does not see sin as the opposite of good, but as something less concrete. 'Sin', she saw, 'has no substance, but is only known by the pain it causes.'

[42]

'Here I saw a great communion between Christ and ourselves, for when he was in pain, we were in pain. And all creation capable of feeling pain suffered with him,' Julian wrote. (*Luttrell (B) f.94*)

But surely there is an absolute distinction between Christ's suffering and our own. His suffering is without sin, and turns into everlasting glory. Our suffering is caused by our sin, and stays as grief and pain. Julian reaches out to a different understanding:

> God showed that sin shall not be a shame to man, but a glory. For just as every sin brings its own suffering by truth, so every soul that sins earns a blessing by love. And just as many sins are punished with much suffering, because they are so bad, even so they shall be rewarded with many joys in heaven, because of the suffering and the sorrow they have caused the soul here on earth.

Revolutionary though it at first appears, Julian's understanding is close to the teaching of the Church. When, on.

[43]

Easter evening, candles are lit from the new-kindled fire, and the Exultet is sung, celebrating the night when Jesus Christ broke the chains of death and rose triumphant from the grave, the words soar up, 'O *felix culpa*': 'O happy fault, O necessary sin of Adam, which gained for us such and so great a redeemer.'

Certainly Julian herself was never tempted to use her insights to set up some new kind of alternative religion, even though there were times when what she had been given to understand seemed to be in direct conflict with the Church's teaching. Julian learnt to accept the truth of both, and was able to rest in the certainty that it was possible for God to reconcile them.

Now, during all this time I had two different kinds of understanding. One was the endless, continuing love, with its assurance of safe-keeping and joyful salvation – for this was the message of all the showings.

The other was the day-to-day teaching of Holy Church, in which I had been taught and grounded beforehand, and which I understood and practised with all my heart. And this was not taken away from me, for I was not turned or led away from it at any point by the showings. But I was taught, by this, to love it and rejoice in it so that, by the help of our Lord and his grace, I might grow and rise through it to more heavenly knowledge and higher loving.

There was a great deal in the teaching of the fourteenth-century Church that Julian had to rise through.

Most of the people in medieval Norwich went in fear of Judgement Day. Painted on the chancel arch of nearly all the churches in the city, where the congregation had no escape from the sight of it, was the 'Doom' – a brightly-coloured picture of the dreadful Day of Judgement.

Money-lenders are boiled in oil, faithless wives are stripped and beaten, imps nip men with pincers, and grinning devils drag the souls of miserable sinners through the jaws of hell into the eternal torment that an angry God decrees for them.

Julian herself accepted that 'one point of our faith is that many creatures shall be damned, as the angels who fell from heaven through pride are now devils. And men on earth who die out of the faith of Holy Church – that is to say, those who are heathens, and also those who have received the Christian faith but live unChristian lives and so die out of love – all these shall be damned to hell without end, as Holy Church teaches me to believe.'

Damnation waited for those who incurred the wrath of God, and the angry Jehovah of the Old Testament thundered for vengeance.

The image of an angry God punishing his people did not disappear with the fourteenth century. A century ago it lay behind the hell-fire sermons of some Victorian preachers and it is the stock-in-trade of their latter-day counterparts, the American television evangelists.

Until recently, all those who received Communion in the Church of England first made their confession in these words – and many still do today: 'Almighty God, father of our Lord Jesus Christ, maker of all things, judge of all men; we acknowledge and bewail our manifold sins and wickedness, which we, from time to time, most grievously have committed, by thought, word and deed against thy divine majesty, provoking most justly thy wrath and indignation against us.'

But Julian's insight, and one that a twentieth-century psychologist would recognise, is that the wrath we see in God is not in him at all, but is a projection of our own anger.

She writes:

For I saw no anger, except on man's part, and God forgives this anger in us. For anger is no more than a perversity and striving against peace and love. And when I saw all this, I needs must grant that the purpose of God's mercy and his forgiveness is to lessen and quench our anger.

For this was shown. That our life is rooted and grounded in love, and that without love we cannot live. And to the soul who by his special grace sees this much of the high, marvellous goodness of God – and that we are forever joined to him in love – it is absolutely impossible that God should be angry. For anger and friendship are two opposites. And so he who quenches and ends our anger must therefore always be loving, gentle and kind – which is the opposite of anger.

For I saw full surely that, wherever our Lord appears, peace reigns and anger has no place. For I saw no whit of anger in God – in short or long term. For truly, as I see it, if God could be angry, even for a little, we should never have life, or place, or being.

So I saw that God is our true peace. He watches over us when we can find no rest, and he works continually to bring us to peace that shall have no end. And when, through the power of mercy and grace, we are made humble and gentle, we are wholly safe. Then suddenly the soul is at one with God, when it is truly at peace with itself, for no anger is found in him.

How did Julian manage to live with the dual knowledge of God's love and the Church's teaching of his wrath? How did she reconcile the irreconcilable?

Julian was able to penetrate to the truth that God is God and that our limited wits, however strenuously and ingeniously we deploy them, cannot search out the height and length and depth and breadth (those meaningless words when applied to God) of his being. As she wrestled with contradictions, she was shown how to rest in the tension between them:

> And, understanding all this, I thought it was impossible that all manner of thing should be well, as our Lord showed me at that time. And I had no other answer from our Lord in these showings except this: 'What is impossible for you is not impossible for me. I shall keep my word in all things, and I shall make all things well.'
>
> So I was taught by the grace of God that I should hold steadfast to the faith, as I had already understood it, and also that I should soberly believe that all things shall be well, as our Lord showed me at that time.

ເ⅊ 8 ᦓᵒᵍᵒ

Father or mother?

Julian reaches a fuller understanding of the connection
between sin and glory in the parable of the lord and the
servant. In the next chapter she develops another thought:
'And so I saw that God rejoices that he is our father,
and God rejoices that he is our mother, and God rejoices
that he is our true husband, and our soul his beloved
wife.'
It is a sentence that brings us skidding to a halt. Ever
since we first learnt the Lord's Prayer we have been familiar with the idea that God is our father. And anyone who
has been to a church wedding has heard Christ described
as the bridegroom and the Church as his bride. But this
is the first time, for most of us, that anyone has suggested
that God is our mother.
An alarming thought strikes us. Can the militant femin-
ists be right? Is God, after all, a woman?
But Julian, who springs this idea on us without any
warning, does not say 'she is our mother', but 'he is our
mother'. What does she mean by it?
As so often in these pages, the best answer is not to
attempt a laborious explanation of what Julian meant, but
to let her speak for herself. The extracts that follow are
from the closing chapters of her book, the fruit of meditation and prayer for more than 20 years.
She begins by seeing motherhood as part of the nature
of the Trinity:

For the almighty truth of the Trinity is our Father –
for he made us and keeps us safe within him. And
the deep wisdom of the Trinity is our Mother, in
whom we are all enfolded. The high goodness of the
Trinity is our Lord, in whom we are enfolded and
he in us.

Then she goes on:

I saw three ways to understand the motherhood of
God. The first lies in our natural making; the second
is Christ taking that nature – and here begins the
motherhood of grace; the third is the work of
motherhood – and in this begins a pouring forth, by
the same grace, of endless length and breadth and
height and depth, of all his love.

In Julian's day, the idea of God as our mother was not
as surprising as it is today. It is our twentieth-century view
of God, focused through the lens held up by nineteenth-
century muscular Christianity and the public school tradition, that has narrowed our vision. We tend to think of
God – Father, Son and Holy Spirit – as an all-male club,
a kind of heavenly Ivy League or Athenaeum. The only
female element has been Mary, mother of God, who is
clearly not in the same category.

To make matters worse, Mary herself, humble, obedient, open to God, has become a focus of controversy and
dissension among Christians. Protestants react vigorously
against addressing prayers to anyone except God himself,
and are shocked by the teaching of the Assumption and
the Immaculate Conception.

The result is that Mary's influence is scarcely felt by
many Christians. She makes a brief appearance at Christmas, kneeling beside the manger, and is packed away
out of sight, along with the shepherds and the wise men,

for the rest of the year. But we cannot understand the nature of God and the nature of his relationship with us, without taking her into consideration.

Julian's perception is that Mary, through bearing Christ, is the mother of us all, but that this motherhood is not hers alone. Above all it is Christ's:

> And so our Lady is our mother, and we are enfolded in her and born of her in Christ. For she who is the mother of our Saviour is also the mother of all who shall be saved by our Saviour. And our Saviour is our true mother, and we shall forever be carried within him and shall never be born out of him.

Our efforts to perceive God will stretch our understanding to its limit, and we shall need everything we can lay our hands on to help us. So it is not surprising that we shall have to think in terms of female as well as male qualities.

Even the awesome God of the Old Testament can be seen in tenderness. The prophet Hosea wrote:

> Thus says the Lord: 'I myself taught Ephraim to walk, I took them in my arms; yet they have not understood that I was the one looking after them. I led them with reins of kindness, with leading-strings of love. I was like someone who lifts an infant close against his cheek; stooping down to him, I gave him his food.'

And Isaiah wrote: 'As a mother comforts her son, so will I myself comfort you.'

Julian recognises that the work of God cannot be discerned only in the male work of creating and begetting. It can also be seen in the women's work of giving birth and of day-to-day care.

'A mother's care is the closest, nearest and surest, for it

[50]

is the truest. This care might never, nor could, nor should, be fully done except by him alone.'

Then Julian reaches deeper and, in a bold image, sees Christ dying in childbirth:

> We know our own mother bore us only into pain and dying. But our true mother, Jesus, who is all love, bears us into joy and endless living. . . And so he nourishes us within himself for love, and he laboured until the full term, because he willed to suffer the sharpest pangs and deepest pains that ever were or ever shall be. And at the end he died.

The death of Christ on the cross, dying so that we might have life, has seldom been more profoundly understood. Julian explores the image further:

> He could die no more, but he would not cease from working. And so he needs must feed us. For the dear love of motherhood has given him a duty to us. A mother feeds her child with her milk, but our beloved mother, Jesus, feeds us with himself. He feeds us courteously and tenderly with the Blessed Sacrament, which is the precious food of life itself.

Yet in all her bold use of images, Julian never implies that Christ is female. Christ is not like a woman, but women, in the special love that comes with giving birth and mothering, are like Christ.

Christ hungered with this loving when he said: 'O Jerusalem! Jerusalem! How often have I longed to gather your children as a hen gathers her brood under her wings!' And the thought is picked up by Julian when she writes:

'This dear and lovely word "mother" is so sweet, and so much itself, that it cannot be properly said of anyone but him, and of she who is the true mother of us all.'

[51]

She goes on, with great tenderness and perception, to develop the insight into how God cares for us:

A kind loving mother, who knows and understands the needs of her child, looks after it tenderly as is her way and nature. And as it grows bigger she changes her ways, but not her love. And when it grows older still, she allows it to be punished, to break it from vice and lead it to goodness and grace. And our Lord does the same thing, truly and well, to those he brings up.

A mother may sometimes let her child fall and be unhappy in many ways for its own good. But she will never allow any real harm to come to the child, because of the love she bears it. And though an earthly mother may have to allow her child to die, our heavenly mother Jesus will not allow any one of us who is his child to perish. For he is all power, all wisdom and all love, and no one is but he.

But often, when our falling and our miserable sin is shown to us, we are so ashamed that we scarcely know where to put ourselves. But our loving mother does not want us to run away from him then, for he does not love us less. But he wills that we behave as children do. For when they are unhappy or frightened, they run quickly to their mother for help, with all their might.

So he wills that we do as a humble child does, saying this: 'My own mother, my kind mother, my dear mother, please pity me. I have made myself unclean and unlike you, and I cannot heal myself without your special help and grace.' And if we do not begin to feel happy straight away, we can be sure he is behaving like a wise mother. For if he sees it is better for us to sorrow and weep, he allows us to be sad for a while, pitying us and sorrowing with us, for love.

Every parent who has brought up a child will know precisely what Julian is talking about. But, if we respond to what Julian says, we may also wonder how it was that she came by the knowledge.

It is time to arm ourselves with our detective magnifying glass and see whether there is anything more that we, or anybody else, can discover about Julian herself.

'This dear and lovely word "mother" is so sweet, and so much itself, that it cannot properly be said of anyone but him, and of she who is the true mother of us all,' Julian wrote. (*Luttrell (D) f.100b*)

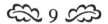

9

The testimony of expert witnesses

In this detective story we are not the only sleuths. The clues we are sifting in our amateur way have already been closely scrutinised many times by professional detectives.

Two sets of clues in particular need a closer look. One set will help us form an opinion on whether Julian was a nun, and hence where she was when she lay gravely ill on 8 May 1373. The other set will help us understand what she means when she says she is 'unlearned' and 'knew no letter' – a claim she makes in both versions of her book.

For by now another version of Julian's book has made its appearance. It turned up eight years after Grace Warrack's edition launched Julian into the twentieth century.

The date was 1909, and the occasion was the dispersal sale of Lord Amherst's library. One of the books he owned was a collection of medieval manuscripts, bound into one volume. And one of the manuscripts was a short version of Julian's book. It begins:

'Here is a vision shown by the goodness of God to a devout woman, and her name is Julian, who is a recluse at Norwich and is still alive, AD 1413.'

The book is much shorter than the one we have been looking at – only 25 chapters long compared with 86. Scholars agree (and we shall not use those words often in the next few pages) that it is Julian's first draft of her book, written soon after the showings on 8 May 1373.

It gives us some extra clues.

When her friends thought she was dying they sent, not for 'my priest' but for 'the parson, my curate, to be at my end. He came with a little boy and brought a cross' (Colledge and Walsh).

She also reports that, as she was contemplating Christ on his cross, 'My mother, who was standing there with the others, held up her hand in front of my face to close my eyes, for she thought I was already dead or had that moment died; and this greatly increased my sorrow, for despite all my pains, I did not want to be hindered from seeing, because of my love for him'.

So now let us see what some of the professional detectives, the scholars and editors, have deduced from the evidence of the text and from their historical research.

Because Carrow Priory had a link with St Julian's church – income from the church went to the priory – and because the nuns of Carrow were known to run a school for young ladies, Grace Warrack comes to the conclusion:

> Julian, no doubt, was of gentle birth and she would probably be sent to the convent at Carrow for her education. There she would receive from the Benedictine nuns the usual instruction in reading, writing, Latin, French, and especially in that Common Christian Belief to which she was always. . . so loyal. . .
> It is most likely that Julian received at Carrow the consecration of a Benedictine nun; for it was usual, though not necessary, for anchoresses to belong to one or other of the Religious Orders.

So, in Grace Warrack's version of events, Julian was a nun and she received her visions in the anchorage in King Street. She was not illiterate, whatever she herself says to the contrary, because she had been taught to read and

'Here is a Vision Shewed be the goodness of God to a devoute woman and hir Name is Julyan that is recluse atte Norwyche and yett is in life Anno dm millino CCCC xiii.' So begins the short version of Julian's book, discovered at a book sale in 1909. (*British Library, Additional MS 37790 f.97*) write by the nuns at Carrow – probably in three languages.

Another of Julian's editors, Clifton Wolters, is more cautious. In the introduction to his Penguin edition in 1966 he says:

> It cannot be said with any certainty that she was a solitary in 1373. Her mother was in attendance, together with other companions, at the illness from which she nearly died, and which was the context of the revelations. The parish priest who came to administer the last rites was accompanied by a child.
>
> Even when allowance is made for the comparative liberty of a medieval anchorhold, the numbers and nature of those present at her putative dying would seem to indicate that she was not enclosed at the time. . .
>
> It might not be too wide of the mark to assume that these revelations were granted to a deeply religious woman living at home, who as a result of them retired to a more perfect way of life – as her contemporaries would see it – as an anchoress. But this is conjecture, not proven fact. Neither is it known if she was ever a professed nun.

But Clifton Wolters entertains no doubts about Julian's ability to read and write:

'She calls herself "unlettered" which with the evidence before us is palpably untrue. . . But the belittling adjective may mean no more than that at the time of the showings she could not read – a defect that was corrected later – or, more probably, that she had no skill in church Latin.'

Next to examine the evidence are two scholars of international repute, Edmund Colledge OSA and Fr James Walsh SJ. In the introduction to their book *Julian of Norwich: Showings* (published 1979) they write:

We have no means of knowing where and how Julian
gained her learning, partly because so little is known
about the facilities for girls' education in her time.
But the evidence of her book points to certain conclusions. From the way in which she associates herself with those who in their youth have dedicated
themselves to the contemplative life, it seems clear
that she had entered a religious order when still
young; if this is so, it must have been there that she
acquired her academic training.

As far as her literary ability is concerned, Colledge and
Walsh are very impressed.

The editors have come to the following conclusions,
guided by their deductions from what she wrote.
Though in several places she protests that she is
ignorant ('lewd') and at the time of the visions she
knew (not, be it noted, 'knows') 'no letter', this is
nothing but a well-known, often-employed rhetorical device, appealing for benevolence from the reader
by dispraising the writer's abilities. The frequently
made statement that Julian was illiterate is a fiction;
she is saying no more than that when she received
her revelations she lacked literary skills, skills which
she later mastered better than most of her
contemporaries. . . Julian became such a master of
rhetorical art as to merit comparison with Geoffrey
Chaucer.

All that she wrote points to her profound knowledge and flexible use of the Latin Vulgate text, and
she seems to have been familiar with a wide range
of the classical spiritual writings that were the foundations of the monastic contemplative tradition of
the Western Church. Her doctrines of the godly will
of the soul, never separated from God by sin, and of

'God our Mother' point to her deep familiarity with
the writings of William of St Thierry . . . And, to
the best of our knowledge, William's writings had
not, at Julian's time, been translated into English.

So for Colledge and Walsh, the nun Julian, whose revelations came to her either in a convent, or in the cell in
King Street, far from being unlettered, is fluent in Latin
and a masterly exponent of written English.

The next detective to scrutinise the clues is Grace
Jantzen, whose book *Julian of Norwich* (published 1987) is
a detailed study of Julian and her theological ideas.

She argues against those scholars who believe that Julian
did not enter her anchorhold until she had finished writing
the long text, at the age of about 52. Having disposed of
them, she goes on:

> However, arguments advanced against her entry into
> the anchorhold only after the Long Text was written
> do point to the likelihood that she was already
> enclosed by the time she composed it. The question
> then arises whether she entered it some time after
> recovery from her illness, or whether she might have
> been enclosed before the illness and the revelations
> took place.

Grace Jantzen does not share Clifton Wolter's doubts
about the secular priest who came to Julian's bedside nor
about the number of people who would be allowed into
an anchorite's cell. It was quite usual for a parish priest to
minister to nuns, she tells us, after the death of so many
clergy during the Black Death, and the other people in
the cell might have been only her mother and her serving
women.

It is the depth and profundity of her prayer life that
convince Grace Jantzen that Julian was already enclosed.

Besides, she asks, if Julian was not an anchoress, what was she?

> Fancy can supply several alternatives. Perhaps, as already suggested, she was a Beguine [a lay sisterhood who took no formal vows]. Or possibly she was a devout woman performing works of social compassion. Or she was a woman who looked after her aged mother until the tables were turned. Or possibly she was a widow, whose husband and children had perished in the Black Death: certainly her tender discussion of motherhood points to some firsthand acquaintance with it – though it might as easily be a reflection backward to her own mother rather than to children of her own. In the end we simply have to say we do not know.

Although Grace Jantzen agrees that Julian may have been educated by the nuns at Carrow, she takes a rather poor view of what they might have been able to teach her:

> Nuns were expected to be able to read and write when they were admitted to a Benedictine convent, but it seems clear that the general standard of education among nuns was declining through the fourteenth and fifteenth centuries. In many English nunneries, the majority knew no Latin, and had to recite their offices by rote.

It was the monks who composed chronicles, while the nuns were expected to do nothing more intellectually demanding than embroider church vestments.

'It would be tempting (though without any foundation in evidence) to indulge the whimsical speculation that this was just what dissuaded Julian from becoming a nun: she had far too keen an intellect to be content to spend her life doing high-class embroidery!' Grace Jantzen writes.

But the evidence of Julian's book, with its references and allusions backwards and forwards, clearly indicate that she wrote it down herself. Her claim to be illiterate could mean that she was able to write only in English and had no formal training in Latin.

Finally we come to the most interesting piece of detective investigation of all. It is carried out by an historian who is also an enclosed nun, Sister Benedicta Ward, and set out in a lecture given in Norwich in May 1988 and published as *Julian Reconsidered*.

If Julian had been a nun, what is there that is missing? She is never mentioned in any existing records of Carrow Priory or any other nunnery. She never refers to her sisters or addresses any remarks to or about nuns or monks; all her concern is for 'mine even-Christians', the lay folk, the holy people of God. She makes no mention of any monastic practices or formation whatsoever and her writings bear no mark of the cloister at all.

Moreover, is it at all likely that a nunnery with such a member, known in her own time as an outstanding counsellor and visionary, would not have done two things: made a fuss to ensure her burial in their grounds and boasted of it; and made sure of having copies made of her Revelations and both keeping them securely and making them available?

The virtual disappearance of her work and the almost total silence about it suggest few copies were ever made, and it follows perhaps that this was because she did not belong inside any settled monastic community with a scriptorium.*

* SLG Press, Oxford, 1988.

[61]

I salute Sister Benedicta as the Sherlock Holmes among literary detectives, capable of making deductions not only from the things that happened, but from the things that did not happen.

' "Is there any other point to which you would wish to draw my attention?"

"To the curious incident of the dog in the night-time."

"The dog did nothing in the night-time."

"That was the curious incident," remarked Sherlock Holmes.'

Sister Benedicta goes on:

> Had she been a nun at Carrow there is one external event which makes it highly unlikely that she would have been able to leave the cloister for the anchorage: in 1369 when Julian was twenty-seven, the plague called the Black Death recurred; of the sixteen nuns at Carrow four died; hardly a moment for the community to agree to the enclosing of another young nun as an anchoress.

The Black Death, Sister Benedicta believes, provides another argument against Julian's being a nun.

> The instinctive reaction after great disasters is towards marriage and childbearing. It was in just such a situation that Julian grew up and no one was to know that the plague would return. At marriageable age [14 or 15] it is most unlikely that Julian would have remained unmarried and there is no reason to suppose that she herself wished for anything else.
>
> The passages in the Revelations that have been alleged to contradict this are, first, her early desire for three gifts of God. . . and secondly by the phrase,

addressed to her by God, 'I thank thee for thy travail and especially for thy youth.'

For the first point, the three wishes are exactly in line with the devout aspirations of lay people of her time and were not confined to novices. The fact that she then forgot about them suggests that they were certainly not for her a determining factor leading to a monastic life; had this been the case she would have built upon them; had they prefaced a life in the cloister they are just the kind of thing a devout little novice might remember and live from. But any pious girl might have thought of just those desires; the piety of her time taught her to do so; but whereas a nunnery would have been the place where she remembered them, marriage, especially happy marriage with the responsibility of a household, might well cause anyone to forget such ideas.

The realities of the fourteenth century meant that 50 was the usual limit of life and 'thirty was middle age, by which time a woman should have been married for at least fifteen years. At thirty Julian fell seriously ill and all she says about her situation fits more easily with the idea of a household than a nunnery.'

In her illness, her bedside was crowded with friends, not sisters; her mother was also there and they were all prepared to laugh heartily. She sent for 'the parson, my curate', a phrase suggesting either a chaplain to a private household or a parish priest, and he came with a boy and a cross. Later she mentions a conversation with a cleric at her bedside, again involving laughter. No abbess or infirmarian seems to have come near her. In place of some mention of prayers at her bedside for a dying nun, Julian says

she wanted to warn those near her bedside to love
God more and leave earthly vanity.

At the end of the Short Text it is Julian's 'even-
Christians' who still occupy her mind. 'God wants
us always to be strong in love and peaceful and restful
as He is towards us, and he wants us to be for ourselves and for our fellow Christians, what he is for
us. Amen.'

I suggest that Julian wrote those words as a young
widow living in her own household with her mother
and her servants.

Sister Benedicta deals just as forcefully with the idea,
held by many scholars, that Julian's ideas of motherhood
came from memories of her own mother:

It has always worried me to think that a woman of
Julian's maturity still held such memories of her own
mother but showed no warmth at all in her solitary
mention of her; in fact her mother totally misunder-
stood her, and attempted to close her eyes when all
Julian wanted was to have them wide open: 'I did
not want to be hindered from seeing because of my
love of Him.'

If it could be permissible to suppose her to have
borne at least one child, as married women should,
all the language of motherhood takes on a new and
natural meaning. . . In 1361, when Julian would have
been nineteen, a form of plague occurred which was
especially fatal to children. . . Had her young husband died either in plague or in war? So many died
of the attacks of the plague and many others in the
wars of the times; and perhaps her child died also?

But it is when she is dealing with Julian's education and
her literary sources that Sister Benedicta comes to the

heart of the matter. Having knocked the opposition all round the court, she writes:

> If there is truth, whether in mathematics or theology, surely it is only sensible to recognise that good thinking can arrive at the same answers independently? There is a kind of presumption in supposing that she could not have possibly thought for herself, that the little lady would need male instruction and had to have books to read. Why not suppose that she thought for years and came up with a startlingly new and immensely cohesive work?

⌘ 10 ⌘

Diligently with candle

The pursuit of truth is a journey into the unknown, but when we get there, the place is familiar.

The truth about Julian must surely be that she was a young widow whose children had died. The idea, once presented, will not go away. We cannot establish it as a fact, but it feels absolutely right.

So, too, does her plain statement that the showings were given to 'a simple creature who knew no letter'. In all that she writes Julian is meticulously, fastidiously, honest. She qualifies any statement that needs it. To suppose, as do Colledge and Walsh, that she was 'appealing for benevolence from the reader by dispraising [her] abilities', simply doesn't ring true. Nor does the suggestion that what she really meant was that she had no skill in church Latin.

If that's what Julian meant, she would have said so. She doesn't beat about the bush.

Julian was given the showings and then had to put her native wit to work. She had to understand what the showings meant, and then, it seems likely, she had to learn to read and write in order to pass it on.

She had no illusions about her qualifications:

'God forbid that you should say or take it that I am a teacher, for I did not mean that, nor never meant it,' she writes. 'I am an unlettered woman, poor and simple.'

And then, knowing she has been given a job to do, she goes on:

> But I know well that what I say, I have it from the showing of Him that is a mighty teacher. And I tell it you for love, for I would to God it were known, and my fellow Christians helped on to greater loathing of sin and loving of God.
>
> But, because I am a woman, must I therefore believe that I should not tell you of the goodness of God, when I saw at the same time that it was His will that it should be known? You shall see in what follows if I have understood well and truly. Then shall you soon forget me, who am of no account – and do so, so that I shall not hinder you – and behold Jesus, who is teacher of all.

You do not have to be a genius to find the truth. We can all get there. But you do have to assess the gifts that God has given you and stretch them to the limit. A high-powered intellect does not necessarily throw more light on the truth than a low-powered one. It all depends on whether the light is beamed in the right direction.

Julian had a very good mind, but not a great one. She did not (in my belief) even know how to read and write when she was given the showings. She had to learn her letters and then tackle the enormous job of passing on to her fellow Christians – in countries yet to be discovered and in centuries she would never see – the message God had given her.

She searched diligently with candle and shed light into the corners of the universe.

With hard work, she was able to learn her ABC and to read and write her native English. But she was light-years away from being able to learn to read and write Latin – the official language of the Church.

And, in any case, what was the point? Her fellow Christians, for whom the message was intended, did not understand Latin. The only time they heard it was when they went to church.

Julian's little house, built against the wall of St Julian's church, was pulled down at the Reformation. This sketch, adapted from a drawing by the architect who restored the church after wartime bombing, shows how it might have looked. (*Tom Hughes; reproduced on cover of 'A Lesson of Love' by Fr John-Julian*)

For in Julian's Norwich, the services in all the churches, and in all the monasteries and convents, were in Latin.

Latin was the scholars' language, the universal language of Christendom. Books were written in it, ideas were exchanged in it. It was spoken as well as written, so that a monk from France or Italy or the Low Couuntries would be as at home in Norwich as he was in his own monastery. And, while Latin was the scholars' language, the aristocracy spoke a language of their own. It was French. For although a week may be a long time in politics, a hundred years was a short time in the Middle Ages. And, when Julian was born, the event that changed England for ever was less than three centuries distant – the Norman Conquest.

Today when we say the words we scarcely realise what they mean, but in sober truth England was conquered in 1066. A foreign invader – with a foreign language – took over the government, the land and the people. The Anglo-Saxon English were defeated.

The Domesday Book is not some kind of quaint historical record. It is the conqueror's account book detailing exactly how much loot he got his hands on.

William, the Norman conqueror, spoke French. The new Norman landlords spoke French. The Norman bishops (among them Herbert de Losinga who set the masons and carpenters to work building Norwich Cathedral) spoke French.

Three hundred years later, in Julian's day, the language spoken at the King of England's court was French – hardly surprising, since Edward III's mother was a French princess, Isabella of France, and his wife, Philippa of Hainault, was Flemish. The language of the élite, and hence the language of international diplomacy, was French.

English was the bottom language in the pile. It was the working language, the language of the streets, seldom used for writing for the very good reason that most of the people who spoke it could not read and write.

English was the language for shouting 'What am I bid for this fine heifer?', for saying 'Tie that knot tight, or that beam will slip and break Jack's neck', for telling your children 'Sit down and shut up'.

If you had any great thoughts, you put them into Latin. If you had any fine feelings, you put them into French.

But the Norman Conquest, although it might have been bad news for the English, was good news for the English language. The conquering Normans did not need to bother to learn the language of the conquered, but, in order to survive, the conquered English had to learn at least a little of the language of their new masters.

But, being English, they did not learn it so well that it replaced their native tongue. They used the new-fangled French words alongside their own sturdy Anglo-Saxon ones until, quite by chance, they had a double set of words at their disposal.

It was not simply that what had been 'pig' and 'sheep' and 'bullock' in the field was transformed into *porc* and *mouton* and *boeuf* when it reached the table.

After the conquest it was possible both to shove and to push, to sweat and to perspire, to hack and to cut. There was a choice between a stench and an odour, between riding in a cart and a carriage, living in a house or a mansion.

To the root stock of the Anglo-Saxon Old English was grafted the graceful flowering of French. It was as if two people produced a child that had the virtues of both and the faults of neither. English became (and I speak as one who is hopelessly in love with it) the most flexible and expressive language in the world.

But even so, in 1373 English was still young as a written language. And when she was given the showings, Julian had not read what few books there were. So, when she was faced with the enormous task of putting what she had been shown down on paper, she had no models – in any language – to draw on.

Chaucer was writing at the same time. But what a difference there was in his background, education and experience – and what a difference it made to his thinking, the language he worked in, and the way he was able to handle it.

He knew Latin (of course) and French and Italian as well. He was continually able to import words and phrases. In the year of Julian's showings he was in Florence and Genoa on a diplomatic mission where he met the great Italian poets Boccaccio and Petrarch. Julian knew only English and for most of her life she lived in one room in Norwich.

When she tells how the blood fell from Christ's head as the thorns pierced it, she can't think back to how Dante would have handled it, or recall a stanza from Virgil. She can only look round the streets of Norwich: 'The great drops of blood fell down from under the crown of thorns like pellets, as though they burst out of the veins. . . The blood was as plentiful as the drops of water that fall from the eaves after a great shower of rain, that fall so thick no one can count them. And they were round like the scales of a herring.'

Julian is proof that the only advice a writer needs is Sir Philip Sidney's to look in your heart and write:

Biting my truant pen, beating myself for spite:
'Fool,' said my Muse to me, 'look in your heart and
   write.'

❦ 11 ❦

A variety of versions

The fact that (as I believe) Julian had no written models to follow, makes a difference to the way her book should be read. Her translator in the Penguin edition, Clifton Wolters, praises her style and her flair, but goes on to say:

'Yet when all this has been said it must be confessed that she can at times be very involved and obscure. There are paragraphs and sentences that could be pruned drastically without loss and given a sharper edge. . . Julian is more obscure than is generally recognised.'

And the new *Oxford Companion to English Literature*, in a sentence that is a masterpiece of imprecision, remarks:

'In general she is not in fact the most appealing of the 14th century English prose mystics.'

I would suspect that some people find Julian is difficult because they expect her sentences to follow familiar written patterns, instead of listening to them as if they were spoken English written down.

This does not mean that Julian's prose is the same as Margery Kempe's dictated chatter. It is the working of a very able mind that has had no formal training in structuring sentences. It reflects, not a Latin-based grammar, but the rhythm of her thinking.

This way of listening to Julian has been captured in the translation *A Lesson of Love* by Fr John-Julian OJN. He sets out Julian's writing in 'sense lines' and uses unconventional punctuation. The result is that you can hear her thinking as she writes.

Clifton Wolters grappled with the problem of Julian's

The interaction of the Father, the Son and the Holy Spirit was very real to Julian. This is how the fourteenth-century artist of the Luttrell Psalter pictured the Holy Trinity. (*Luttrell (J) f.44*)

repetitions. This is part of her chapter 54:

> For the almighty truth of the Trinity is our Father:
> he makes us and preserves us in himself; the deep
> wisdom of the Trinity is our Mother, in whom we
> are enfolded; the great goodness of the Trinity is our
> Lord, and we are enfolded in him too, and he by us.
> We are enfolded alike in the Father, in the Son, and
> in the Holy Spirit. And the Father is enfolded in us,
> the Son too, and the Holy Spirit as well: all mighti-
> ness, all wisdom, all goodness – one God, one Lord.

It does sound extremely complicated, and one can well
understand Clifton Wolters ringing the changes with 'too',
'alike' and 'as well' in an attempt to lighten it, itching to
reach for the pruning knife.

But listen to the same passage from *A Lesson of Love*:

> The all Powerful truth of the Trinity is our Father,
>   for He created us and keeps us within Him;
> and the deep Wisdom of the Trinity is our Mother,
>   in whom we are all enclosed;
> the exalted Goodness of the Trinity is our Lord, and
>   in Him we are enclosed and He in us.
>   We are enclosed in the Father,
>   we are enclosed in the Son
>   and we are enclosed in the Holy Spirit;
>   and the Father is enclosed in us,
>   and the Son is enclosed in us,
>   and the Holy Spirit is enclosed in us:
>   all Power,
>   all Wisdom,
>   all Goodness,
>   one God,
>   one Lord.

When Julian is read like this, the repetitions which Clifton Wolters describes as 'turgid' shine out from the page as clear as a candle in darkness.

This passage from chapter 20, when Julian saw Christ on the cross, also becomes clear when set out in this way:

> And thus I saw our Lord Jesus lingering on a long time
>> [for the unity of the Godhead gave strength to the manhood out of love to suffer more than all men could suffer].
>>> (I mean not only more pain that all men could suffer, but also that he suffered more pain than all men of salvation who ever were from the first beginning until the last day, could measure or fully imagine – considering the worthiness of the most exalted, honourable King and the shameful, spiteful, painful death – because He that is most exalted and most worthy was most fully brought to nothing and most utterly despised.)
>
> The most significant point that can be seen in the
>> Passion is to comprehend and to understand
> that He who suffered is *God* –
> seeing beyond this two other points which are
>> lesser
>> (the one is *what* He suffered,
>> and the other is *for whom* He suffered).

Here is a series of complex and inter-related thoughts which Julian puts down on paper as they come to her. The clarity of her thinking is obscured when her prose is written down in a solid chunk and punctuated conventionally. Once the phrases are broken into their separate ideas by short lines, dashes, brackets (both square and round) and italics, her meaning is crystal clear and the rhythm of her thinking is apparent.

Julian can seem difficult, and it is possible to get bogged down in her book. But, when this happens, the fault in my view lies not with Julian but with the translation. I have found myself having to come up for air when reading Julian via all the previous translations. But when I first laid hands on a copy of *A Lesson of Love*, I read it cover to cover in one sitting.

So why, you may ask, have I not used it when quoting from Julian in this book?

The main reason is that, because of the way it is laid out, it simply takes up too much space. The second is that the translation I have used is already familiar to people who have met Julian through *Enfolded in Love* and *In Love Enclosed*. And the third is that, being mine, I feel more at home with it than anyone else's.*

I hang on to it because, for me, it has got something of the strength and texture of the native homespun material about it. For, while I delight in the magical tapestry of English and the rich threads and colours that French and Latin and Greek have woven into it, I am always conscious of the sturdy Anglo-Saxon canvas backing into which it is stitched.

* *All Shall Be Well* by Sheila Upjohn (Darton, Longman and Todd, 1992).

12

A lesson of love

Julian came to know God through being in his presence. But up to now we have almost ignored the fact that, when she first found herself in Christ's presence, it was at the most agonising moment of his life on earth. She shared, as she had asked, Christ's suffering on the cross.

Nowadays we are sheltered from death and from physical suffering. Death takes place out of sight in hospitals. People who are injured in accidents are bundled quickly into ambulances to be taken away and taken care of. There is no blood in our streets.

The public hangings and the executions (whether by axe or by guillotine) that used to be the high point of every public holiday have been replaced by the letting of stage blood on television. The bloody heads of aristocrats no longer roll into the basket at the feet of Mme Defarge as she sits knitting. The falling corpses she watches today will get up and walk away when the filming is over.

So most of us have no idea what it is like to see a man tortured to death.

For crucifixion is horrific. First the lashing, so that the flayed skin is running with blood. Then dragging the heavy crossbeam through the streets to where the upright stands ready. Then the nails hammered in through hands and feet.

It is a slow death. It took Christ six hours to die.

Death, when it comes, is from exposure, loss of blood,

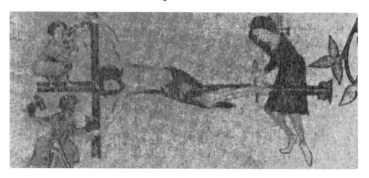

Julian saw the crucifixion as clearly as if she had actually been there.
'The huge, hard, hurtful nails pulled the wounds wide open,' she
wrote. This picture from the Luttrell Psalter shows the nails being
hammered home. (*Luttrell (A) f.93b*)

dehydration and suffocation. The unsupported weight of
the hanging body bears down on the chest so the lungs
can no longer expand.

Julian was there, and she saw it all.

That day when our blessed Lord and Saviour died
upon the cross there was a dry, frosty wind that was
bitter cold, as I saw it. . . And although the pain of
it was sharp and bitter, it was also long drawn out,
as I saw it, and agonisingly dried out all the living
essence of Christ's flesh. . .

The blessed body hung alone and dried there a
long time, and the nails wrenched it as the weight of
the body pulled against them. For I understood that,
because of the softness of the tender hands and feet,
the huge, hard, hurtful nails pulled the wounds wide
open. And the body sagged with the weight of its
long hanging.

And there was piercing and wrenching of the head,
and the binding of the crown of thorns – all caked

[78]

with dried blood with sweet hair twined in it – dried
flesh sticking to the thorns and thorns to the dying
flesh. . . I did not see how the wounds were made,
but I understood it was by the sharp thorns, and
the way the crown was crammed on, roughly and
harshly, hard and without pity. . .

As for the pains that I saw, all that I can say is too
little, for it cannot be talked of. . .

This showing of Christ's pains filled me full of
pain, for though I knew well he suffered only once,
yet it was his will to show it me and fill my mind
with it, as I had often asked before. Then I thought:
'I little knew it was what pain I asked for,' and like
a fool regretted it, thinking that if I had known what
it would be like I should not have prayed to suffer
it. For I thought this pain was worse than death itself,
my pain. . . .

This much, we may think, is predictable. We may ever
feel a twinge of anxiety in case Julian, in sharing this
suffering so vividly, is about to become either morbid or
hysterical. But at the point of death, everything changes

I looked for the moment of his death with all my
strength, and thought to have seen his body quite
lifeless, but I did not see him so. And just at the same
moment, it seemed, that I thought that life could last
no longer and the sight of his end must be shown,
suddenly, as I looked on that same cross, his
expression changed to joy.

The change in his blessed mood changed mine,
and I was as glad and merry as can be. Then our
Lord brought this gladly into my mind: 'Where is
any part of your pain and grief now?' And I was
overjoyed.

[79]

Whatever we had expected, it was not this. We are used to feeling sorrow at the crucifixion, and joy at the resurrection. Joy in the crucifixion itself is something most of us have never looked for. On Good Friday we acknowledge our guilt and our shame:

Who was the guilty? Who brought this upon thee?
Alas, my treason, Jesu, hath undone thee.
'Twas I, Lord Jesu, I it was denied thee:
I crucified thee.

But, having accepted our responsibility, we do not often take the leap forward to understand that it was not our sin that forced Christ to suffer. He chose to suffer of his own free will, because he loves us. Julian goes on:

Then our good Lord Jesus Christ said: 'Are you well paid by the way I suffered for you?' I said: 'Yes, Lord, I thank you. Yes, good Lord, blessed be your name.'
Then said Jesus, our kind Lord: 'If you are well paid, I am well paid, too. It is a joy, a happiness, an endless delight to me that ever I suffered my Passion for your sake. If I could have suffered more, I would have suffered more. . . '
And I looked with great diligence to know how many times he would die if he could, and truly the number was so far beyond my understanding and my wits that my mind had not the strength or space to comprehend it. And when he had died as many times as this, yet he would still think it nothing for love. . . Every day he is ready to suffer again, if it could be.
For if he said he would make a new heaven and a new earth for love of me, this would deserve little in reward, for he could do this every day, if he so

[80]

wished, without any toil or trouble. But to die for love of me so many times that the number is too huge to reckon, this is the highest offer that our Lord God can make for man's soul, as I see it.

We all of us have been taught that God is love. Julian understands what that means. We struggle to love God because we ought to, and because this is the first and great commandment. But Julian recognises that God does not have to make an effort to love us. He has always loved us, and will always go on loving us more than we are able to comprehend or to imagine.

In the final chapter of her book Julian sums up the essence of what she has been told in all the showings. It is as moving as it is simple:

And from the time that it was shown, I often asked to know what was our Lord's meaning. And fifteen years after and more, I was answered in inward understanding, saying this:

'Would you know your Lord's meaning in this? Learn it well. Love was his meaning. Who showed it you? Love. What did he show you? Love. Why did he show you? For love. Hold fast to this and you shall learn and know more about love. But you shall never need to know nor learn anything else for ever.' So was I taught that love was our Lord's meaning.

And so I saw full surely that before ever God made us, he loved us. And this love was never quenched, nor ever shall be. And in this love he has done all his works, and in this love he has made all things profitable to us, and in this love our life is everlasting.

In our making we had beginning, but the love in which he made us was in him from without beginning, in which love we have our beginning. And all this shall we see in God without end.

✿ 13 ✿

Beyond words

Many people have first come to know Julian through finding her words in T. S. Eliot's poem 'Little Gidding', the final poem of *The Four Quartets*:

> And all shall be well and
> All manner of thing shall be well
> By the purification of the motive
> In the ground of our beseeching.

It ends with these lines:

> And all shall be well and
> All manner of thing shall be well
> When the tongues of flame are in-folded
> Into the crowned knot of fire
> And the fire and the rose are one.

Having discovered her in T. S. Eliot, they go on to discover what she has to say in the rest of her book.

We have looked at her perception that God and man are intricately knitted together, that there is no wrath in God, and that God does not blame us for our sin. What else is there that she can teach us?

Julian spent her life in meditation and prayer. But prayer, like the concept of sin, is something that has gone out of fashion. Not many people, I would guess, begin and end their day with a prayer, and to pray for more than a few minutes at a time, except in church, would these days be considered eccentric.

And, in any case, what are we supposed to say? There's the Lord's Prayer, of course, but surely we ought to add something of our own? And while it is all very well to beg God to help us when someone we love is dangerously ill, or when a hurricane is blowing, what on earth are we supposed to pray about apart from that?

The most obvious way seems to be to make a list of things that need attention – wars and famines, illness and death, treachery and violence, people we know are ill or in trouble – plus all the contents of the television news and the newspaper headlines, so that at least God is aware of what is going on and that we are concerned that he should be doing something about it.

Of course we know that God knows about it already. But Julian's insight is that it is God who puts the prayers into our mind. God told her:

'I am the ground of your beseeching. First it is my will that you should have this; then I make it your will, too; then I make you ask for it, and you ask. How then should you not have what you pray for?'

But we all know that we do not always get what we ask for. We beg that a friend may recover from illness – and he dies. We ask for success in exams – and we fail. We beseech God that we should be loved – and love is taken from us.

Julian's answer is that we must reach into what is happening, and discern God's will in it. Through God's love we are able to come to terms with bereavement, with failure, with rejection and to recognise that no place is so dark or so painful that God has not been there before us and stays there with us; that there is no evil so bad that he will not turn it to good.

[83]

Our blessed Lord answered very gently, with a most kind look, and showed that Adam's sin was the worst harm that was done and ever shall be until the world's end. And he also showed that this is clearly known by all Holy Church on earth.

More than this, he taught me I should look on the glorious Atonement. For this making amends is more pleasing to God and more helpful for the salvation of many, without compare, than ever the sin of Adam was harmful.

What our Lord means by this teaching is that we should remember this: 'Since I have brought good out of the worst evil, I want you to know, by this, that I shall bring good out of all lesser evils, too.'

We must trust God as we pray: 'Some of us believe that God is all-powerful and is able to do everything, and that he is all-wise and knows how to do everything – but that he is all love and will do everything, there we hold back. In my view nothing hinders God's lovers more than the failure to understand this.'

We can safely leave the practical results of our prayer to God. Its real importance is that it draws us closer to him.

When we are in danger and distress and we cry 'Help me, God,' it does not bring God nearer to us. He is always closer to us than our own soul and never leaves us. Julian wrote:

> For when the soul is tempest-tossed, troubled and cut off by worries, then is the time to pray – so as to make the soul willing and responsive towards God. But there is no kind of prayer that can make God more responsive to the soul, for God is always constant in love. . . God's goodness is not caused by our praying.

It hardly needs saying that, if we could change God's mind and make him do what we want, it would be a disaster. The purpose of our prayer is to come into God's presence so that he can make our will one with his.

Julian's own prayer, when she prayed to experience Christ's Passion, was in these terms:

> Lord, you know what I desire, but I desire it only if it is your will that I should have it. If it is not your will, good Lord, do not be displeased, for my will is to do your will.

But if we know that God already has everything in hand, why should we bother to ask him for anything? As we look round the world, there may seem a lot that needs praying about, but if God is in charge and all shall be well, there doesn't seem much point in trying to contribute. Julian writes:

> He looks on us with love and wants to make us his partner in good deeds. And so he leads us to pray for what it is his pleasure to do. And he will reward us and give us endless recompense for these prayers and our goodwill – which are his gifts to us.
>
> God showed such pleasure and such great delight, as if he were much in our debt for every good deed that we do – and yet it is he who does them. And because we ask him eagerly to do the things he loves to do, it is as if he said: 'What could please me better than to ask me – eagerly, wisely and willingly – to do the very thing I am going to do?' And so, by prayer, the soul is attuned to God.

And there is another reason, too:

> Our prayer makes God glad and happy. He wants it and waits for it so that, by his grace, he can make

us like him in condition as we were by creation. This is his blessed will. So he says this: 'Pray inwardly, even though you find no joy in it. For it does good, even though you feel nothing, see nothing, yes, even though you think you cannot pray. When you are dry and empty, sick and weak, your prayers please me, though there be little enough to please you. All believing prayer is precious to me.'

Because of the reward and endless thanks he longs to give us in return, he is avid for our prayers continually. God accepts the goodwill and work of his servants no matter how we feel.

But prayer is not summed up by asking for things – the prayer of petition. There is also the prayer of contemplation – of resting in God's presence.

It is a way of praying that is the antidote to the frenetic 'doing' of our century, when we are all supposed to rush madly about being outward-going, outward-looking and extrovert.

Contemplative prayer is a way of looking inwards – not inwards into the confines of a stifling ego, but inwards and beyond to the silence that is God.

There sometimes seems in these days to be, not a conspiracy of silence, but a conspiracy against it. Mindless music babbles at us in offices, in factories, in restaurants, in pubs. It even seeps from the walls of supermarkets. It is as if we dare not be alone in silence for fear of what we may find there.

And indeed silence, where we hear the breathing of our own fears, our inadequacies, our emptiness, can be horrifying. But it is in the silence that we shall find ourselves and in that silence, too, that we shall find God.

Julian wrote: 'The best prayer is to rest in the goodness

of God, knowing that that goodness can reach right down to the lowest depths of our needs.'

Words do not matter. You may repeat 'Lord, have mercy' or 'Abba, Father' as you kneel in prayer. But the heart of contemplative prayer is: 'Be still and know that I am God.'

It should come as no surprise to us that contemplative prayer is coming back into fashion. We have too many words these days. Every day brings a torrent of words pouring out of radio and television. Every day brings a dead weight of newsprint – most of which is thrown away unread. Every day brings an avalanche of junk mail and computer print-outs.

In the beginning was the Word, but we have overproduced and trivialised words to such an extent that, in order to find the Word at the heart of the universe, we have to take the way of silence.

Many religious orders report that, although numbers are falling in communities that are active in teaching and nursing, contemplative communities are growing in strength. A new contemplative order, which is dedicated to Julian of Norwich, has been founded in the United States.

These contemplative orders are also attracting oblates – men and women who keep the rule of the order in the world beyond the cloister walls. The hard shiny surface of materialism is beginning to crack as the long-stifled seed of the spirit sends up shoots.

We shall never be able to feed all the hungry, clothe all the naked, comfort all the dying, cure all the sorrows of the world. But we can enter into all this through prayer and, entering, bring it before God. The pathways of prayer lead to unforeseen destinations.

Back to the beginning

It is beyond reason that a book written by an uneducated woman in a back street of Norwich 600 years ago should have grown to have such influence in the last decades of the twentieth century. Yet it is so.

This book was published 16 years to the day from the 600th anniversary celebration of Julian of Norwich in Norwich Cathedral on 8 May 1973. It was that celebration that started Julian's influence spreading like a flame through stubble.

But since so few people had even heard of Julian then, where did the idea for the celebration come from?

I have a letter from an enclosed nun which reads:

> You might be interested to know that the idea for the sixth centenary celebrations originated here in a casual conversation at our Community recreation. Three of us were professed on May 8th 1966. Near that date in 1972 we mentioned that next year would be the 600th anniversary, and our chaplain said, 'We must do something about that. I'll get in touch with the Dean of Norwich who is my friend.' And thus it began – one of God's providential acts.

In Norwich today, the Julian cell is full of silence. There is no bustle, no chatter, no consulting of guidebooks. People do not come here to look, to see or to be seen, they come to kneel where prayer has been valid.

Outside in the garden there may be laughter and picnics.
Inside the cell is silence and peace. There is a comradeship
in the silence that cannot be put into words. There is a
shared perception of the peace.

In practical terms not a vestige of Julian remains. In
spiritual terms she is everywhere.

Julian tells us to forget her – 'then shall you soon forget
me, who am of no account, and do so, so that I shall not
hinder you' – and she has seen to it that we do.

She has no enshrined relics, no known grave. Her cell
was pulled down at the Reformation. St Julian's church,
with its little Saxon tower, was badly damaged when it
suffered a direct hit in an air raid in 1942.

The church as it stands today is almost entirely rebuilt,
and Julian's cell itself is completely new. It was built (on
what are believed to be the original foundations) only in
1952. The Norman archway at its entrance comes from
another church. There are no externals to worship.

Yet in this place Julian found a window that opened
onto heaven. It is open still.

> O do not look for Julian here
> Her cell's been empty half a thousand years.
> Only the words she wrote remain
> And shine through darkness like a flame.
>
> Her life was bound by walls of stone
> In one small room she lived alone
> And yet she found a window there
> Through which eternity shone clear.
>
> If you'd find Julian, look with faith
> Until her form begins to fade.
> Look through her as a window pane
> To see God's love is written plain.

Give thanks for Julian and her book
And let us wisely learn to look
That we forget the one who held the pen
And see God's love that ransomed men.

Tailpiece:
'My dear sisters, you should keep no beast except a cat,'
warns a rule book for anchoresses written in
Julian's day. (*Luttrell f.16b*)

Postscript

St Julian's church, where Julian lived and wrote her book, still stands on its original site. After the war, with the church bombed and the surrounding area derelict, it might have been left ruined, particularly since Norwich already has 32 surviving medieval parish churches.

It was the sisters of The Community of All Hallows, Ditchingham who inspired the restoration and ensured that it was carried out.

Today St Julian's is open every day from dawn to dusk. Julian's rebuilt cell is a place of silence and prayer where the Eucharist is celebrated and the Offices are said every day. There is almost always someone on hand in the church or in the All Hallows house next door to share a problem or give advice.

Retreat groups can stay overnight at All Hallows, but many people make the cell the centre of a day retreat. The Friends of St Julian's form a prayer link with the shrine, and there are Julian Meetings throughout the country – groups which meet for meditation and silent prayer.

Thanks to royalties from books, there is a library of spiritual reading that reaches out to other faiths and which also aims to include everything published about Julian.

Julian would have known Norwich Cathedral, where the retable that her bishop, Henry Despencer, gave in thanksgiving for his defeat of the Peasants' Revolt is still in use as an altarpiece.

There is a stained-glass window of Julian in the Bauchon chapel and another in St Saviour's chapel. Just inside the south door is a chapel dedicated to St Catherine which is designed for meditation and silent prayer.

St Julian's church is a short drive or ten minutes walk away from the cathedral. Details of Friends of St Julian's, Julian Meetings and retreats from: The Julian Centre, St Julian's Alley, Rouen Road, Norwich, NR1 1QT; Tel. 01603–767380 (11am–3pm weekdays).